*European Integration
and Immigration
from Third Countries*

Grete Brochmann

European Integration and Immigration from Third Countries

With a Foreword by
Astri Suhrke

SCANDINAVIAN UNIVERSITY PRESS

Oslo – Stockholm – Copenhagen – Boston

Scandinavian University Press (Universitetsforlaget AS)
P.O. Box 2959 Tøyen, N-0608 Oslo, Norway
Fax +47 22 57 53 53

Stockholm office
SCUP, Scandinavian University Press
P.O. Box 3255, S-103 65 Stockholm, Sweden
Fax +46 8 20 99 82

Copenhagen office
Scandinavian University Press AS
P.O. Box 54, DK-1002 København K, Denmark
Fax +45 33 32 05 70

Boston office
Scandinavian University Press North America
875 Massachusetts Ave., Ste. 84, Cambridge MA 02139, USA
Fax +1 617 354 6875

ISBN 82-00-22721-9

Published with a grant from the Research Council of Norway

Design: Astrid Elisabeth Jørgensen
Cover illustration: Albanian refugees proudly present their newly obtained
          passports upon arrival in Italy 1990.
          © AFP/NTB-foto
Typeset in 10.5 on 12.5 point Photina MT by Engers Boktrykkeri A/S, Otta
Printed on 90 g Carat Offset by Engers Boktrykkeri A/S, Otta, Norway

"The more fiercely a civilization entrenches itself, the less it is left with to defend."

Hans Magnus Enzensberger

Foreword

A striking feature of the migration debate in contemporary Europe is the vehemence with which governments and citizens deny that their states, in contrast to the USA, Canada, and Australia, are immigration countries. Yet this is evidently a case where «the lady doth protest too much». In fact, Europe west of Russia and the Ukraine now has about the same proportion of foreign-born persons as the United States and Canada together. Also Norway has an immigration rate which belies its self-image as a country of overwhelmingly home-grown citizens. The gross immigration rate in Norway in the early 1990s was about 0.3 per cent per capita (excluding asylum seekers), or equivalent to the per capita rate of the principal immigration country in the modern world, i.e. the United States.

Why have these facts been obscured or denied? Of course, it can be argued on grounds of terminological purity that the word «immigration country» has less to do with rates of migration than with the policies adopted by the receiving states towards migrants: some seek to attract and settle foreigners, others emphasize exclusion. But the denials suggest more complex processes. Those who know may be afraid to publicize the facts lest they encourage restrictionist, xenophobic movements. Others may fear, to the contrary, that adjusting self-image to reality will justify more liberal policies towards immigrants and refugees, since proponents of the latter can legitimately ask whether, as an already existing country of immigrants, there is much to fear by admitting more. Behind these questions, in turn, are profound issues of collective self-identity and the associated insecurities and fears, pride, and hope that run deep in the national psyche of modern nation-states.

Given the subject matter, a wide-ranging and fearless discussion of European immigration policies will necessarily touch on issues that are controversial, and may be misused. But these questions are already in the public arena, are often misused sometimes with violent consequences and loss of life and there is a pressing need for dispassionate analysis to balance the debate.

Brochmann's book is a timely contribution. Focusing on the harmonization of European policies towards third-country citizens, she shows how national policies are formed by pressures that are simultaneously conflicting and reinforcing: on the one hand, nation-states experience increasing demand from migrants and asylum seekers for entry; on the other, the integration dynamic in the European Union requires progressively greater harmonization of regulations governing both entry and treatment of non-Union nationals. As Brochmann shows, the rationale for individually restrictive policies are based in part on legitimate considerations of the interests of existing members of the collectivity, but in part on unfounded fears about labour displacement and other dislocations. Yet the logic of harmonization on contemporary Europe suggests that each state emulate the policy of the least liberal member of the Union, or, all other things being equal, accept a disproportionate part of the demand for entry. As a result, a progressively restrictive common policy towards third-country nationals has developed.

The question of control goes to the heart of this policy debate. Immigration control is as modern a concept as the nation-state. When individuals were subjects and not citizens, they could and did trade sovereigns with considerable ease.

The concept of citizen, by contrast, denotes a community of members who possess rights and obligations. Hence the question of access to the community becomes central, and, in periods when demands for entry exceeds the supply, so to speak, becomes critical. The current notion of a migration crisis goes beyond Europe's hesitant transformation from a sending to a receiving region. Also in Canada, Australia, and the United States has there been a perceptible concern recently to increase controls and reduce immigration. The perceived crisis reflects a number of factors, the most important of which are related to structural economic change and high levels of long-term unemployment in the industrialized states, powerful «push factors» rooted in inequality and demographic pressures in the South, and the revolutionary technologies of communication which facilitate global travel and networking. The result is that Northern industrialized countries find themselves facing painful dilemmas: tighten control but at the cost of sacrificing some civil liberties and economic vitality; relax control but court a political backlash and uncertain economic consequences at home; control immigration by picking the best manpower, but leave the sending countries worse off by draining their most skilled people. The question of illegal migration is particularly vexing not simply as a control issue, but as a fundamental normative dimension which concerns the legitimacy of the state and the nature of a society where a significant proportion may be «non-members» without formal status and legal rights.

Arguably, immigration policies will always have an element of «managing uncertainty», as a recent Carnegie endowment study of the subject is entitled.* The policy dilemmas can nevertheless be softened by more knowledge that will inform and improve the management of migration process. Critically important knowledge relates to the topics examined in this book: the historical context of current migrations, assessments of

---

* D.G. Papademetriou and K.A. Hamilton, *Managing Uncertainty: Regulating Immigration Flows in Advanced Industrial Countries*, Washington, DC 1995.

present migration trends, examination of dynamics of integration (versus marginalization and repatriation), and of the socio-economic consequences of immigration in receiving countries.

Chr. Michelsen Institute, Bergen
October 1995
Astri Suhrke

Preface

This study has been facilitated by the generous support of a number of individuals and institutions. Without being able to acknowledge each by name, I would like to mention the many informants in research milieus, in the state/federal administration in various EU countries, and in the European Commission. Special thanks, in this respect, go to the *Groupe d'Etude des Migrations et des Relations Interethniques* at the *Université Catholique de Louvain* in Belgium, where I spent one and a half years as a guest researcher from January 1992 till June 1993. I also wish to thank the most helpful staff at the European Commission/DG5/Freedom of Movement and Migration Policy Division, where I spent a few months doing "fieldwork" in 1992. My stay in the Commission gave me invaluable access to documentation and information as well as informal discussions with various staff members. In this context, I especially wish to thank Mrs Annette E. Bosscher (Head of Division) who received me in such a friendly way.

Financial support has been provided by the Research Council of Norway, through a three-year full-time grant. Here, let me express my gratitude to the board of the research programme *International Migration and Ethnic Relations* for both financial and professional support.

Finally, I am grateful to my research colleagues at the Institute for Social Research, among them particularly Fredrik

Engelstad, Aud Korbøl, Lars Mjøset and Mariken Vaa, who have given constructive comments on earlier versions of this book.

Oslo, October 1995
Grete Brochmann

Contents

Introduction

In today's world, when more people travel than ever before, many of us will probably at some point have reflected on the existential coincidences of birth place and nationality. We may well also have felt a bit uneasy over the enormous gaps in life chances that derive from these coincidences of fate. According to Benedict Anderson, "it is the magic of nationalism to turn chance into destiny" (1992:12). This destiny presents us with a serious reality in Western Europe today. Thousands of people from the "Third World" – people whose life chances have been restrained because of structural factors – are appearing on the European doorstep every day.

This is perhaps the most fundamental quandary that comes to mind. It touches upon a central normative principle of international relations: the principle of universal human rights. Yet another, often conflicting, normative principle has been gaining ground in the domain of immigration lately: this is the principle of national sovereignty. On the one hand, international conventions and agreements serve to protect the individual from persecution, and guarantee the right to protection of basic human rights. On the other hand, restrictive regulations intended to keep out major parts of the migration flow have become increasingly more pronounced in the Western world.

A changing immigration regime

During the post-war period up till the early 1970s, immigration played a central role in the development of Western Europe. Migrant workers contributed significantly to the industrialization and the creation of the working classes on the Continent, indeed, the development of the prosperous economies of the West has depended heavily on immigrants.

All the same, neither states nor populations were much concerned about migration for the first 25 years after the Second World War. More recently, however, a collective consensus has developed to the effect that immigration from certain parts of the world represents a major security threat in today's Europe. Sometimes immigration is even seen as heir to the military enemy image from the period of the Cold War.[1] Why has this significant change taken place? When did immigration turn from an asset to a burden in the public discourse?

The argument is here that a combination of three sets of factors can help to explain this change. Firstly, economic factors: The assumption that immigration has developed into an economic burden on the receiving states is a basic explanatory factor. Secondly, political factors: European integration on the one hand, and the fall of the iron curtain and the end of the Cold War on the other, have reinforced restrictive attitudes and actions undertaken against immigrants. Thirdly, national identity factors: The new "identity squeeze" where the promotion of European integration from "above", and increasing immigration from "below", exert a dual pressure on established national identities in Europe.

Increased immigration has coincided with substantial unemployment and a significant restructuring of the economies of Europe. The need for excess labour has currently diminished significantly. Moreover, immigration to Western Europe has changed character, partly as a response to the restrictive policies of the receiving states since the 1970s. Today's new

---

1. See Sciortino 1990; Weil 1992 and Garcia 1992.

immigrants are perceived basically as an economic burden on public budgets. Politically speaking, great changes have taken place in Europe in the last few years. Political blocs have become eradicated, power constellations redefined and new tensions engendered through intra- and inter-statal processes. The West is characterized by a movement towards economic and political integration, with reduced control for the nation-state, whereas the East has witnessed the downfall of an empire through nationalistic mobilization. Slumbering ethnic conflicts are again awakened by the sudden openness and transitory character of the situation, and the question of legitimacy of national borders has again come to the forefront.

These profound changes have also had a migration corollary. The impression has been created that a new era of migration is in the making. The new situation has induced a crisis atmosphere, further aggravated by the tragedy of Yugoslavia.

The opening of East–West relations, in combination with the already existing uneasiness over immigration in many of the EU[2] countries has created new conditions for immigrants from the poorest parts of the world. This applies both to those who already live within the EU region, and to those who are knocking at the gate.

The new pressure from the East came at a time when the number of asylum seekers as well as the unauthorized (illegal) immigration from poor countries in the "South", had reached high proportions in many EU member countries.

There is yet another dimension: the supra-national integration process within the European Community. This process – a major challenge to questions of sovereignty and national regulations as such – also has far-reaching implications for migration, immigration control and the rights of foreigners. With the Single European Market immigration issues have

---

2. I will generally use the terms "European Union", "EU", and the "Community" except in cases where I am referring to conditions prior to the establishment of the Union.

come high on the political agenda – higher than most politicians had expected a few years ago. After years as a marginal political topic, immigration has developed into one of the most central and most complicated issues within the Community. The *transitional* atmosphere that currently predominates in Europe, both in relation to the recent opening towards the East, and as a result of the supra-nation-building process within the European Union, may disturb the traditional basis for identity in the area. This involves subtle mechanisms which are hard to trace empirically, but which might nevertheless have a bearing on attitudes towards foreigners.

The EU dimension

Protection of national borders and labour markets are not new issues. Border control regarding citizens of other countries has long been a central aspect of the sovereignty of nation-states. With the establishment of the European Single Market in 1993, this is, however, no longer solely a national consideration. The promotion of mobility of labour, one of the pillars of EU philosophy, may also mean that the preconditions for control of "third-country nationals" (citizens from non-member countries) are basically changed. The open internal frontiers in the Single Market may imply that anyone entering a member country from outside the Union, will have free access to all the other member-states. Thus, the weakest link in the chain may, as a port of entry, define the control of the influx to the Union as a whole, unless control with "third-country nationals" is somehow maintained.[3] Besides, to prevent variation in immigration policies (welfare benefits, social status, political rights, possibilities for citizenship etc.) from making some member countries more attractive to immigrants than others, a move for harmonization of these issues seems very likely.

---

3. This issue has been one of the major stumbling blocks in the EU discussions on immigration, and agreement has not yet been reached.

Harmonizing immigration policies in Europe has, however, proved to be a difficult undertaking indeed. Because immigration control in a broad sense is so closely attached to the issue of national sovereignty, social and labour market policy, it emerges as a basic stronghold of the nation-states in the integration process.

The immigration issue illustrates a general dilemma facing the EU countries in the intersection between the national and the inter- (supra-) national level: new structures are to be formed in a field which is touchy at the national level. On the one hand, the EU countries want to establish a common internal market, removing internal borders in order to promote competition and growth. On the other hand, the nation-states also cling to sovereignty in connection with control of their own conditions, in this case their own frontiers.

The main thrust of this book is to describe and analyse the dynamics between the various EU member-states and the Community in the development towards a common immigration policy. There is a striking contrast between the economic, social, and political significance of migration, and the degree to which it has been subject to international organization. It is the hypothesis of this work that the cooperation there is, has been generated *negatively*, in the sense that mutual dependence defines the level of necessary cooperation among the states. In this book, the intersection of the analytical level of the nation-state and the Community will be in focus, with the emphasis on *political dynamics*. In essence this is a study on the preconditions for the development of a common immigration policy within the European Union. Without analysing all the member countries as such, examples from some of the countries will be used to illustrate the strategic dilemmas confronting the Union on its way to a tentatively harmonized immigration policy. France and Germany will in this respect appear most frequently, as they are the two most significant states in terms of immigration to Europe – numerically, politically and historically. Also some non-EU Western European countries will appear occasionally, for illustrative purposes.

Analytical dynamics and unit of analysis

Immigration has basically been a *national* preoccupation. Entry control, possible welfare benefits, as well as control over the institution of citizenship have been guarded by national governments, even though international and supra-national conditions increasingly constitute essential parameters of the field. States in Europe no longer represent independent and self-reliant entities, and the general international integration has made an impossibility of isolated national policies. Besides, international migration has challenged the traditional conception of nationhood, and made the nationally defined population a somewhat outdated concept. Also *studies* of these phenomena have by and large been bounded by nation-state thinking. According to Anthony Giddens, this is partly due to an internal bias in the sociological discipline: What is the object for research is internal processes in societies where external boundaries are taken as given. "The nation-state . . . is the sociologist's society" (Giddens 1985:172). This bias which seems to be even stronger within the discipline of *political science*, may nevertheless inhibit new perceptions of current developments and processes. Existing analytical instruments may fail to apprehend emerging structures.

However that may be, more research energy should be channeled across the established state borders and into the dynamics between states, beyond the traditional units of analyses. Reality provides an ample basis for this supplementary orientation.

In this book the main unit of analysis will be the *political process* towards the harmonization of immigration policies in the area of the European Union. The book will analyse international mechanisms of conflict and cooperation that serve to form policies at a national and now tentatively also at a supra-national level. The question of *control* will be central, in terms of "institutional mediation of power" (ibid.:9). Non-control and the incapability/incapacity of effectuating this mediation of power will be as relevant in this context. Such non-control or unsuccessful control can, in Giddens' view, be studied partly through a mechanism he calls "dialectics of control": "All strategies of control employed by superordinate individuals or groups call forth counter-strategies on the part of subordinates" (ibid.:11). The forces that influence the *effectiveness* of policy implementation will consequently also be subject to analysis in this context.

In other words, it is the question of *preconditions for control* that represents the major focus here. In this approach one needs conceptual means to understand the conditions for change in terms of structure and agency. "Agency" will in this study refer basically to an aggregated level – through institutions, organizations, networks or groups of individuals. *Immigrants* will be used as a broad category including the whole range of groups most relevant for Western Europe today: settled foreign labour, temporary workers, relatives of original migrants (immigration through family reunification arrangements), unauthorized immigrants, refugees, and asylum seekers.[4] Structures are to be found both nationally and inter/supra-nationally, the two major ones being the labour market and established policies on various levels. The processes to be studied are rooted in the interaction between the structures and the actors. As with individual action, institutional action or group action is in this context seen as governed by an interplay of motivational factors and structural conditions in a concrete context. Time, space, and society, broadly speaking, influence the actor, and are *reflected* in the actor; likewise the actor *feeds back* into society, and hereby reproduces and/or transforms it. In this way, society continuously represents *living* historical aggregates, where yesterday's actions become today's

---

4. For both principal and political reasons it is problematic to include refugees and asylum seekers in the immigrant category. Nevertheless, since the aim of this book partly is to analyse the interconnections between the various streams, and the unforeseen consequences of governmental policies related to influxes of foreigners generally speaking, it is more convenient to use the label "immigration" *en bloc*. The central qualitative differences between the various groups will become apparent in the analysis.

context for conscious behaviour. In the decision-making process, constraints and facilitators will influence this interplay. A central objective here is to identify the structure of some of these constraints and facilitators; furthermore, to analyse how and why progress in the harmonization process is hampered. What are the major conflicting interests, and what are the different possibilities for various actors to promote their claims? What are the possible and likely constellations of action in efforts to promote or hinder structural change? What are the major conflicting strategies for adaptation to the new European context?

These problems will be analysed through a simple model of the Western European nation-state contained in a dynamics where control policies, integration efforts and labour market parameters interlink in a complex web. The concrete composition of the triangle (Figure 1) in terms of the internal distribution of strength between the three fields in operation will constitute the immigration order of each country. On the other hand, this dynamic composition will, in the West European

Figure 1. European integration and the nation-state complex of immigration control

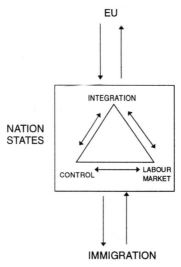

context of today, also influence the space for manoeuvre for other European countries, and for the European Union as such. Thus, Union member-states are today under pressure from two sides: from "below" in terms of increased immigration, and from "above" through the drive towards European integration and the convergence of immigration policies. A methodological problem in studying the European integration process is that the object is a rapidly moving target. A whole range of parallel processes is running simultaneously, partly with their own logic, partly influencing each other. The scholar constantly runs the risk of being outdated. This problem has tentatively been tackled by placing analytical emphasis on historical preconditions, current political mechanisms, and prevalent tendencies, more than empirical descriptions on a day-to-day level.

The structure of the book

The first chapter will introduce the issue of immigration control in relation to the questions of national sovereignty, nation-building and nationhood. The welfare state is analysed as an additional dimension in this respect, confronting modern states with dilemmas in the interface between humanitarian principles and vested interests on behalf of the citizens.

The second chapter gives a brief historical account of the post-war setting: the economic and political forces behind the policy changes of the 1970s.

The third chapter presents the factual background to the specific immigration setting in Europe today. Where do the migrants come from? What are their motivations? What kinds of policy responses have European governments produced? What are the prospects for future immigration, and how can these be analysed?

The fourth chapter deals with the process towards convergence/harmonization of the immigration policies of the EU member-countries: motivational forces, constraints and contradictions.

Chapters 5, 6 and 7 analyse the internal dynamics of each member-state in the interplay between control policies, integration endeavors and labour market variables, as sketched in Figure 1.

The final chapter pulls together the various strands of the analysis, concentrating on a juxtaposition of national and supra-national processes.

Chapter 1

Immigration Control and Nation-States

Immigration control – a recent phenomenon

Until the First World War, few political and legislative barriers hindered the international movement of persons. It was possible to travel through Europe, and even overseas, without a passport. Even the settlement of people in new countries involved few bureaucratic formalities. Immigration from poor countries in the South – from colonies or elsewhere – had never seemed a realistic possibility, until transport and communication facilities underwent significant improvements in the beginning of the 20th century. Immigration control in the modern sense is a fairly recent phenomenon.

Until the EU integration process accelerated and the "crisis" perception of immigration took form in Western Europe, immigration policy had basically been a *national* preoccupation. Scholars have tended to view immigration control nearly as an intrinsic part of the development of the modern nation-state. According to Michel Massenet,[5] a state ultimately "ceases to be a state if it does not control the implantation of foreigners on its soil" (quoted in Freeman 1979:209). It seems necessary to add that the context in which immigration takes place is essential to how governments conceive of the phenomenon. The development of the modern nation-state had

---

5. Director of the Population and Migration section at the French Ministry of Labour, and a central actor in the formulation of immigration policies in France 1962–68.

progressed far before it appeared necessary to introduce immigration control in any comprehensive way.

Tomas Hammar (1990) divides the history of migration in Europe into four periods, the first starting with the huge wave of overseas emigration from Europe from the middle of the last century and onwards. During this first phase leading up to World War I, international travel was not controlled in Europe, with the exception of Tsarist Russia. Economic liberalism made unhindered flows of merchandise and people possible. It was even possible to settle down and work without the formality of permits.

The second period (1914–1945), was characterized by the introduction of a system of regulation and control. This was the first time that economic depressions with severe unemployment led to protectionist demands from the national labour forces.

The third phase, starting in 1945, was again a period of a relatively liberal regulation policy in Western Europe. The post-war reconstruction with extensive labour demand provided the economic rationale for this liberalism. Cold War refugees and the decolonization process also accounted for parts of the positive immigration spirit in Europe during these years.

The fourth period, signified by the "immigration stop" of the early 1970s, again introduced strict immigration regulation throughout the "receiving" countries of Europe (ibid.: 42–44). This re-introduced restrictionism has been further strengthened (although with some contradictory effects – see later) during the 1980s and 1990s.

Ever since the last century, free movement of people has remained an ideal, although it could not always be pursued, due to extraordinary circumstances. Even the "immigration stop" of the 1970s was originally presented as a *temporary* ordinance. After the last recession in the late 1980s, combined with increasing immigration pressure from East and South, this ideal may well have been abandoned – but, paradoxically, at the same time as the free movement of labour is instituted as a cornerstone in the European Union.

National integration

Ernest Renan stated in his famous Sorbonne speech in 1882, *"Qu'est-ce qu'une nation?"*, that the essence of a nation is that all individuals have many things in common, and also that they have forgotten many of those things.[6] Such amnesia in relation to immigration is a striking example of this. Statistics reveal that every fourth Frenchman has foreign parents or grandparents (Silverman 1992:3). Apparently this also holds true in Germany (Dittgen 1992). Hans Magnus Enzensberger describes this socio-psychological phenomenon by saying, "people conceal and disown their own nomadic origins as soon as they have claimed a territory. In order to justify their claim, they have to forget about their past" (Enzensberger 1992:15).

Immigration control appears to serve a dual function: manifesting sovereignty externally, while maintaining the sociocultural confines internally, thereby sustaining the political backing and integration of the nation-state (Freeman 1979; Zolberg 1983).

The question of national *integration* is essential in the continuous nation-building process, and it represents the same duality as the nation-state itself. It serves the "politics of identity" and the "politics of interest", in Rogers Brubaker's words (1992:188). A certain level of national integration is necessary to get the economy to function, and it is likewise necessary to make people identify with forces beyond themselves and their closest community; to create a society where individual contributions tune in with the larger group, which is "imagined" and constituted as the nation. As Brubaker points out, *state interests* cannot be delineated solely in terms of economic, demographic and military considerations. Interests are also mediated by cultural terms: through self-understanding and by ways of "thinking and talking about nationhood"

---

6. *"Or l'essence d'une nation est que tous les individus aient beaucoup de choses en commun, et aussi que tous aient oublié bien de choses"* (referred in Anderson 1992:5ff).

(ibid.:16). Ernest Renan made a similar distinction: "A community of interest is assuredly a powerful bond between men. Do interests, however, suffice to make a nation? I do not think so. Community of interest brings about trade agreements, but nationality has a sentimental side to it; it is both soul and body at once; a *Zollverein* is not a *patrie*" (Renan 1990:18).

The process of integration will vary in intensity, depending on the historical context, with the most significant (so far) being the stage of nation-state formation. The socio-political entities we today see as nations were constituted largely through the rise of modern states as they "expanded and delimited their territories, enhanced their capacities for administration, and constituted their inhabitants and subjects as citizens" (Calhoun 1992). This initial formation process was in many places carried out as a response to external threats: to interstate rivalries. Internal unity was formed by mobilizing against external enemies.

The duality of external/internal forces in creating social cohesion and a feeling of identity is today relevant in Europe, in a new and somewhat paradoxical fashion. The cross-national integration of the European Union, with the transfer of sovereignty from the nation-state to a higher body, is provoking a revitalization of the *national* integration process in many places. The term "integration" thus can denote a dual and contradictory process in the current European context. A society can open up towards other societies as an act of integration, or it may close itself off from the outer world as an, internally speaking, integrative act (Østerberg 1988).[7]

Furthermore, the increased immigration pressure from third countries has added another dimension to the integration complex: immigrants are commonly seen as external individuals and groups who should (or should not) be integrated *into* "fixed settings", i.e. established and rather "completed"

---

7. The classic study of this mechanism where an external threat promotes internal cohesion is Durkheim's "Le suicide" from 1897, where the Jews became an integrated group precisely through the hostility and polarization of their surroundings.

cultures. National identity seems, more than anything else, to be based on the ability to construct *difference* and specificity in relation to others: the uniqueness of "us" compared to "them". Thus, a part of the "instrumental passion" (Kitching 1985) of nationalism is to use images of the others to construct the self-imagination. According to the Danish social scientist, Ulf Hedetoft, this conception of *difference* may mean that sovereignty can be re-erected as a forceful and national idea detached from the official political life of Europe. In essence, by weakening the borders between "them" and "us" at one level, distinctions seem to reappear with increased strength elsewhere (Hedetoft, in *Information*, 18 September 1992).

Initial integration processes took place in varying ways among the European nation-states. France and Germany are often cited as opposite poles; France as the ideal-type founder of the nation-state phenomenon, through its 18th-century revolution and the subsequent centralization/state formation process; Germany as a latecomer with the central state "added on top" (Calhoun 1992) of a number of regions.[8] The way in which integration and national identity formation took place through the nation-building process may have an important bearing on today's immigration and naturalization policies, as hypothesized by several scholars.[9] Historical heritage and national symbolism greatly contribute to the political discourse on immigration control and "aliens" policies.

From the perspective of the nation-state, migration can be seen as a disturbing factor in the nation-building process. According to Max Silverman, migration of goods and people has exposed an inherent instability of the alliance between the nation and the state, "an alliance built on shaky foundations ever since the former was constructed according to the retrospective illusion of unity and continuity, whilst the latter

---

8. The classic work here is Ernest Renan's "Qu'est-ce qu'une nation?" ("What is a nation?") written in 1882 (Renan [1882]1990).
9. See, e.g. Silverman (1992) and Brubaker (1992).

was always prey to economic and other forces which did not respect national frontiers" (Silverman 1992:35).

The idea of the nation as historically and culturally distinct, with the state as its 'natural' political and territorial framework, has put emphasis on cultural or ethnic *homogeneity*. Membership in a given political and national community was made dependent on cultural conformity. Although there is much to be said about the empirical evidence concerning the link between ethnic homogeneity and successful integration (USA being the most common example of nation-building in a non-homogeneous society), the ideology has served a function in its own right historically speaking. According to the (non-liberal) ideal of the nation-state, people should stay where they were born, provided this was their "natural" environment.

Historical experience has shown that profound differences in people's living conditions, as well as political conflicts of various kinds, uproot people, and set them in search of safer grounds, in a broad sense. Against the background of the ideological emphasis placed on the cultural homogeneity factor, it seems reasonable in modern nation-states to expect some kind of regulation or control of potential and actual flows of people, not least when more and more people are grasping at the possibilities offered by easier and cheaper transport. The *formal* right of border regulation, it seems, has so far never been waived by modern states, although many modifications have been accepted in terms of bilateral agreements and international conventions.

Citizens and denizens

The ultimate control or the innermost gate in relation to "aliens" is represented by the institution of citizenship. Every modern state delineates its citizenry by establishing who belongs and who does not. Through this dual inclusion/exclusion exercise, the members of the state are identified, and their rights and duties sorted out accordingly. The modern state secures legal equality for its members, which means equal access to the benefits of the state, and equal political, civil and social rights (Layton-Henry 1990). Citizenship is, however, not a pure reflection of rights attached to residency. It provides, when achieved, a persisting personal status, independent of temporary or prolonged absence. The modern state thus serves as an enduring "membership organization" (Brubaker 1992:21).

The EU integration in combination with rising immigration pressures has led to a revival of *membership in nation-states* as a political theme. The question of "what it means and what it ought to mean to belong to a nation-state" (Brubaker 1992:188) has come to the fore. With the internal market, citizenship in one state opens up access to other states in the Community in terms of right of entry, residence and work. Therefore the core of the nationality issue – membership in one state – is suddenly of importance for the other member-states as well. Yet the question of citizenship still lies entirely within the jurisdiction of each and every state, "last bastion of sovereignty", as Brubaker puts it (ibid.: 180).

Tomas Hammar has made a distinction between *foreigners* (temporary workers and political refugees), *denizens*[10] (permanent residents without full citizenship) and *citizens* (1990). By the end of the 1980s there were about 13 million non-citizens in Western Europe (excluding the UK), of whom 60 per cent were denizens (Garcia 1992). By and large, these denizens have access to the same social and civic rights as citizens, but they lack the right to vote.[11]

Due to the existence of the category *denizens*, some scholars seem to consider citizenship less important today (Soysal 1993; Brubaker 1992). Others, like Marie (1991), and Hollifield (1992), see restrictive naturalization policies as a chal-

---

10. Again, among denizens, one could designate a *scale* as to statuses/privileges enjoyed by immigrants: For example, legal permanent residents, political refugees, other EU-nationals.

11. An exception is the right to participate in municipal and county elections in Sweden, Norway, the Netherlands, and Denmark.

lenge to democracy and the notion of equality.[12] Both groups nevertheless agree that citizenship is highly significant at the symbolical level. The question of nationhood and belonging, as the cultural/psychological counterpart of citizenship, has indeed gained importance in the European context. In terms of identity, national citizenship is reasserted, even though the European states are extending social and civic rights to their foreign populations. According to Soysal (1993), the two basic elements of citizenship, identity and rights, have in fact become *decoupled* in the post-war era.

Immigration and the welfare state

National integration and boundary control gained an additional dimension through the growth and development of the modern welfare state.

Historically, the welfare state developed in close alliance with the nation-state, although the "end result" varies throughout the world. Civil, political, and social rights developed within specific states that granted and protected them. The welfare state evolved basically into a closed system where the individuals who "agree to share according to need, have to experience a sense of solidarity that comes from common membership in some human community" (Freeman 1986:52). Yet at the same time, the modern welfare states necessarily constitute relatively open economies in terms of trade relations, mobility of capital, services and – to a certain extent – labour. The development of the welfare state can, in Gary P. Freeman's view, be seen as a "dialectic between the distributive logic of closure – mutual aid undertaken by members of community according to socially defined conceptions of needs – and the distributive logic of openness – treatment according to one's performance in the marketplace without re-

---

12. In areas of high foreign density, as in the larger European cities, one quarter of the inhabitants often do not have citizenship. This implies that they cannot participate in political decisions, even though they pay tax and are legally established in any sense of the term.

gard to membership status or need" (ibid.). The crucial issue in such a closed system is, of course, citizenship. No *international* system has ever provided similar rights or benefits. The unequal development of the world is marked by vast differences in power, wealth and welfare for the people. Access to goods and rights for members of the fortunate societies requires the exclusion of "the others". To quote Joseph H. Carens: "Citizenship in Western liberal democracies is the modern equivalent of feudal privilege – an inherited status that greatly enhances one's life chances" (Carens 1987:252).

The welfare state brings a dual dimension into the migration context: On the one hand it becomes pertinent to control the limited benefits of the welfare societies; on the other hand, the welfare aspect makes it more attractive to enter from "the other side". As Aristide Zolberg puts it: "The collective good component of income helps explain why the tendency to move from poor to rich countries is somewhat independent of a given labour market conjuncture in the place of destination, why the supply of foreign labor tends always to outrun the demand for it, why many who set out as migrants strive to become immigrants, and especially why, in the final analysis, all relatively advantaged countries must adopt restrictive immigration policies to protect their advantages" (Zolberg 1983:37).

The discussion on migration and the welfare state is nevertheless not all that simple: If we set aside the fact that even among the fortunate citizens of the "North", access to benefits is often differentiated, the presence of immigrants in the welfare societies may have complex effects. It might be argued that the very presence of cheaper labour facilitates the sustenance of many welfare provisions (in terms of services) in times of economic recession. It is also frequently maintained that immigrant labour provides a net economic benefit to the rich states of the "North", considering demographic dimensions, taxes, favourable effects on inflation etc. (see, e.g. Castles 1986; *Migration News Sheet* December 1991). Gary P. Freeman, however, argues that a mesalliance is created between employers and indigenous labourers in welfare societies in letting immigrants take jobs in the lower segments of the labour market – jobs which the citizen workers do not want. Social benefits facilitate this, even in periods of unemployment: Citizen workers can choose not to move or to take up jobs below or outside their skill area. The employers on their side can have a cheap supply of labour, by ignoring social costs. This is in turn the kind of situation which Ottar Brox (1991) and others have pictured as the basic long-term threat to welfare society at large: the disturbance of the regulated labour market, with the consequent undermining of the political consensus which forms the backbone of the welfare state.

There is no unitary "impact of immigration". Skill levels of immigrant groups vary significantly among host countries, and there may be marked differences between labour market segments *within* national economies (see Salt 1992; Barsotti and Lecchini 1992). According to both aggregate and case studies, the economic effects of immigration are generally positive, yet there is no clear consensus as to the impact on *economic restructuring*. Immigrants may prevent or postpone a further recession in declining industries, but they may also help new industries to expand. The argument against the use of low-paid immigrant labour in this respect is that its presence prevents the restructuring required in certain industries to keep them competitive (Salt 1992). Concerning the "net result" for the nation-states, research does not give any clear message as to the balance between tax paid and welfare benefits received. According to various studies, it seems that immigrants pay less in taxes, but also receive less in welfare.

This discussion will not be further elaborated on, as the calculations tend to become highly complicated.[13] The point here is that the (European) welfare states *act* as if immigration is a

---

13. According to Freeman, "one is free to believe more or less what one wishes about the economic impact of migration because the facts are so much in dispute" (Freeman 1986:60).

threat to society[14] – at least under the current economic and political conditions. Consequently, in political terms, immigration poses a notable challenge to the legitimacy of the modern welfare state: real or perceived immigration pressure may lower the backing of those strata which used to constitute the major basis for welfare policies. At the same time immigration is used by nationalist forces to mobilize against political protagonists for welfare state policy. The parallel process of increased immigration and the erosion of welfare state provisions may start interacting, at least at the level of ideology and popular perception. The serious dilemmas which confront welfare states in this realm will be discussed later in the book. Let us now look back into the recent history of European immigration to detect trends and experiences that can cast light on the current situation.

---

14. The USA, Canada, and Australia together represent an interesting contrast to Western Europe when it comes to public attitudes towards immigration. Although these countries are subject to many of the same economic setbacks as Europe, increased (legal) immigration appears to be public policy (see Livi Bacci 1991; and OECD Observer 1992:21).

Chapter 2

Post-War Immigration to Europe

Post-war labour demand

By and large, immigrants are appreciated if they contribute
more than they cost, in economic, social, demographic and cultural terms. Although the blend will vary from country to country, it is usually the economic dimension that dominates the cal-
culation (Entzinger and Carter 1989). Any "cost-benefit" consideration of immigration is, however, highly contextual.

There is no such thing as a universal measure of *absorption
capacity*, as, e.g. the French "threshold-of-tolerance" approach
might imply.[15] Israel has received two million immigrants (out
of now approximately five million inhabitants) since 1948, on
the basis of religious criteria. Some Gulf countries have max-
imized the economic profits of cheap labour to the extent that
foreigners outnumber citizens. Germany received more than
12 million immigrants during the first years after the Second
World War, etc. And likewise, today's variation between OECD
countries in Europe on the one hand, and the USA, Canada,
and Australia on the other, illustrates the contextual significance of the term "absorption capacity".

During the Second World War, millions of people were up-
rooted and put on the move from war zones and occupied territories. When the war ended there were fears that the various

---

15. This "seuil-de-tolérance" debate is discussed in greater depth in Silverman
(1992).

European countries would not have the capacity to absorb these destabilized populations, some ten million altogether (Hammar (ed.) 1985). These fears appeared to be unfounded. War-stricken countries had lost large numbers of their able-bodied men and the period of post-war reconstruction required vast stocks of labour.

Labour demand in Central and Northern Europe was so extensive that as early as in the late 1940s major migration began from Southern Europe (primarily Italy) moving towards the North-West. Initially Sweden and Switzerland were the major receiving countries, followed by England and France. During this period, lasting up till the late 1950s, around 50 per cent of all labour migrants came from Italy. From the late 1940s onwards, France had also started actively recruiting labour from Turkey. Germany was, during the first 15 years after the war, almost completely engaged in including several million Germans from the East: both those expelled as a result of the war, and a constant flow from the DDR (Rystad 1992). West Germany accepted refugees and people who had been forced to leave former German-speaking areas, territories which after the end of the war belonged to other states. The erection of the Berlin Wall in August 1961 discontinued the influx of labour from the East, making the question of alternative sources a pressing issue for the German economy.

France, by now concerned about demographic shortcomings, took on a more active recruitment policy. Plans were made for large-scale immigration. The official recruitment agency, ONI (*Office National d'Immigration*), however, never came to play the dynamic role which it was intended for, and France ended up accepting spontaneous immigrants in the same way as the other West European countries of immigration.[16] Furthermore, employers became directly involved in recruiting labour, particularly during the 1960s.

---

16. French relations with Algeria provided an additional source of labour, as the country was, until independence in 1962, constitutionally a part of France. This meant that Algerian workers (and their family members) were French citizens.

The comprehensive reconstruction of Europe following the war engendered rapid economic growth. Economic liberalism was again the leading line of thought; it implied that international migration, both in terms of recruited labour and spontaneous immigrants, were welcomed as a means of stimulating the economy.

Also other factors led to an increased need for immigration during the post-war period. Improved educational facilities and the general growth optimism that accompanied the new era increased job expectations, and started an upgrading of jobs for native workers. Thus, the "labour-shortage" theory has to be qualified by a more political dimension. According to Gary P. Freeman, the extent to which indigenous labour supply is considered adequate or not is at least partly a question of labour organization among the native workforce. Their ability "to oppose capital-intensive modernization, production speed-ups, and shift work, and to avoid certain tasks altogether, contributes to employers' perceptions of labour scarcity" (Freeman 1986:56). Thus, the supply of labour is, to a certain extent, a result of negotiations between capital and labour.

However that may be, foreigners gradually became a structural component of the West-European labour market, with immigrants slowly occupying certain sections of low-skill, low-salary, dirty and often dangerous jobs in construction, manufacturing and the service sector. In some places, firms could run their expanding businesses without making structural changes, thanks to the abundant supply of cheap labour. Investment in modernization was often put off in favour of continued production with labour-intensive methods. On the other hand, new investments were sometimes made possible by the profits generated by the large supply of foreign labour (Hammar 1985).[17]

Generally speaking, there seems to have been a clear connection between migration and economic growth during the

---

17. There is certainly variation within this general picture, between various countries on the one hand, and between sectors of the economy on the other.

post-war years. Many scholars seem to think that the "German Miracle" had not been possible had it not been for large-scale immigration. On the other hand, economic expansion also *generated* immigration.

It is also worth noting that, despite the extensive waves of immigration in both France and Germany, there were hardly any negative public reactions to this policy in the 1950s and 1960s (Hollifield 1992).

From asset to burden?

A new phase in the European political economy of migration started in 1973 with the oil crisis and the subsequent deep recession.[18] A major economic restructuring process was set in motion, and this process appeared to be long lasting. The Western economies were confronted with inflation and unemployment at the same time, and the growth rate approached zero. Modernization and rationalization of industries became the remedy throughout Western Europe. These efforts partly implied a decrease in dependence on foreign labour. The structural change in this respect was particularly notable in France, where the foreign labour component had grown significantly during the late 1960s and the early 1970s.

The oil crisis was the major occasion for introducing a strict immigration regulation in the early/mid-1970s, popularly known as the "immigration stop", in most Western European countries. Germany was first in the field, introducing the new regulations in November 1973, followed by France in June 1974 (Rogers 1985). There were, however, other reasons for this policy change beyond purely economic ones.

---

18. In fact there seem to have been many interacting reasons for the termination of what has been termed the "golden age" of 1950–1973, of which the oil embargo is only one. Angus Maddison argues for four major factors in this respect: 1. the collapse of the Bretton Woods fixed exchange rate system; 2. the erosion of price constraints, and the emergence of strong inflationary expectations as a prime element in wage and price determination; 3. the shock of a tenfold rise of oil prices; 4. the erosion of exceptional supply-side factors (Maddison 1991:177).

In France the period of decolonization from 1958 to 1962 introduced a massive and basically uncontrolled immigration. Average annual immigration leaped from 66,400 in the period from 1946 to 1955 to 248,800 during the years from 1956 to 1967. Alongside this major increase, administrative control over foreign labour was decreasing (Hollifield 1992). Thus, even before the "stop" was introduced, French authorities had instigated a change in policy. Early in 1972 a *circulaire* (with the power of an executive order) was issued, aimed at eliminating all types of non-contractual labour, preventing the exploitation of foreign labour, and re-establishing control over the migration process. Immigration to France had also undergone a substantial change during the late 1960s in terms of representation of nationalities. Again, according to Hollifield, the source of "highly assimilable Southern European Catholics" had begun to dry out (with the exception of Portugal), and non-European, mostly Muslim, immigrants had begun to take their place (ibid.:58). These new attempts to curb the immigration flow were, thus, directly linked to the rising unpopularity of Third World immigration. It was during this period, 1972–74, that the first symptoms of a nationalist reaction against immigration appeared (ibid.:69).

Whereas the 1960s in France were characterized by fairly uncontrolled immigration, the tendency in Germany was towards gradually stronger control. The equivalent to the French ONI (*Office National d'Immigration*), the *Bundesanstalt für Arbeit* (BA), was the most important institution for managing foreign-worker recruitment. By the late 1960s this institution was handling more than 70 per cent of all recruitment in West Germany. Work permits were seen as contracts not only between the employer and the worker, but also between the worker and the state. The state made it an obligation for employers to provide immigrant workers with adequate housing. Family reunification was discouraged. Although the German authorities were more successful than their French counterparts in controlling immigration during the late 1960s and the early 1970s, the number of foreign workers was increas-

ing. As in the case of France, there was also in Germany growing concern about social and political consequences of large-
scale immigration in the years prior to the "immigration
stop".

Consequently, the oil crisis, followed by a lasting recession,
inaugurated a policy change that most likely would have appeared sooner or later anyway. The increase in immigration
had grown out of control, and it was becoming politically untenable to sustain labour recruitment in the face of rising unemployment. Increasingly immigrants were seen as competi-
tors for scarce jobs, social goods, housing, etc. There was also a
prophylactic element in the policy change. The authorities
had witnessed a tendency towards more long-term settlement
of those who were believed to be only "guest workers". These
long-term residents had acquired rights that made them less
expendable in times of recession. This meant that the "buffer"
function of the foreign labour system did not work as intended. By introducing a recruitment stop, one could at least
put a brake on further settlement.

With the "stop" the receiving countries intended to admit
only those immigrants who had specific qualifications to fit defined needs in the labour market – in addition to some family
members of already established immigrants, as well as a fixed
quota of political refugees. The two last categories have been
admitted on humanitarian grounds.

Western Europe and control policies since the 1970s

European immigration policies since the early 1970s have
been based on the assumption that it is possible to put an effective halt to immigration.

In fact, the "stop policy" has *not* been a success as such in
any of the countries in question, and several *unforeseen conse-*
quences have appeared. Migrants have, as a group, influenced
the recipient countries in ways that were not planned, and

which now in turn constitute the basis for policy making within the European Union.

First and foremost, the recipient countries had always thought that the influx of foreign workers was to be a *temporary* phenomenon – and this invariably proved to be wrong. Migrants recruited during the growth period until the early 1970s, have so far chosen to stay; moreover, they have to a large extent brought their families with them. The registered growth in foreign population after the "recruitment stop" is not constituted by new labour, but by family members of those already immigrated, through the right to "family unification" or through reproduction (births). This is the case in all Western European countries. The restrictions in themselves have presumably implied that immigrants already inside the EU region would not risk leaving the area, for fear of not being allowed re-entry. The restriction thus may have implied that migrant workers who would, under a less restrictive immigration policy, have travelled back and forth periodically, instead decide to settle down in Europe together with their closest kin.

Secondly, the *kind* of immigration that dominates in each country seems in part to be a function of the policies followed by that country's authorities. The potential migrant would (if he or she has any choice) figure out which queue is most strategically feasible.[19]

The costs for the state vary according to type of immigration. The recipient country may consequently be confronted with irrational macro-effects of policies originally intended to reduce immigration. In trying to limit *labour* migration to a minimum, a country may find that the much more expensive *asylum-seeker* queue is growing.[20] The most inexpensive type

19. In Spain the number of asylum seekers fell after introduction of the regularizations of illegal immigrants (Commission of the European Communities 1992a).

20. While *labour* migrants were in demand, numerous actual refugees from the Third World came to Europe as *de facto* job seekers or students, as immigration control was fairly loose (Blaschke 1989). This was occasionally also the case with labour migrants from Greece, Portugal, and Spain during the period of dictatorship.

Table 1. Foreign resident population in Western Europe, 1950–90 (in thousands, with percentage of total population)

Country	1950 No.	1950 %	1970 No.	1970 %	1982* No.	1982* %	1990 No.	1990 %
Austria	323	4.7	212	2.8	303	4.0	512	6.6
Belgium	368	4.3	696	7.2	886	9.0	905	9.1
Denmark	–	–	–	–	102	2.0	161	3.1
Finland	11	0.3	6	0.1	12	0.3	35	0.9
France	1765	4.1	2621	5.3	3680	6.8	3608	6.4
Fed. Rep. of Germany	568	1.1	2977	4.9	4667	7.6	5242	8.2
Greece	31	0.4	93	1.1	60	0.7	70	0.9
Ireland	–	–	–	–	69	2.0	90	2.5
Italy	47	0.1	–	–	312	0.5	781	1.4
Liechtenstein	3	19.6	7	36.0	9	36.1	–	–
Luxembourg	29	9.9	63	18.4	96	26.4	109	28.0
Netherlands	104	1.1	255	2.0	547	3.9	692	4.6
Norway	16	0.5	–	–	91	2.2	143	3.4
Portugal	21	0.3	–	–	64	0.6	108	1.0
Spain	93	0.3	291	0.9	418	1.1	415	1.1
Sweden	124	1.8	411	1.8	406	4.9	484	5.6
Switzerland	285	6.1	1080	17.2	926	14.7	1100	16.3
United Kingdom	–	–	–	–	2137	3.9	1875	3.3
Total**	5100	1.3	10200	2.2	15000	3.1	16600	4.5

* 1982 is a reference year, rather than 1980, since the data are better for 1982.
** Includes interpolated figures for the missing (–) data.
  Source: Fassman and Münz 1982, referred in Stalker 1994

of immigration in the short run – temporary labour without dependents – may on the other hand have detrimental effects on society – through pressure on wages, social dumping, ethnic tension, etc. This form of immigration could be the most attractive for some employers, albeit untenable for the unions; in the end it might contribute to undermining labour-market planning as such. The catch for the Western European countries in this respect is that a more costly kind of immigration has coincided with an economic recession, a fact which seems to be structurally connected in the first place.

Thirdly, the existence of restrictive policies throughout Europe has made marginal differences between potential receiver countries even more important as to the relative "pull" forces towards immigrants. This, in turn, may engender cumulative processes, as in the case of Germany, with its (until 1993) liberal asylum policy.

Fourthly, certain sectors of the economies were still in need of foreign labour. Tougher economic conditions will often tempt employers to hire illegally: The use of cheap foreign labour has become an important means for small and medium sized firms to retain some flexibility and lower production costs in a competitive situation. An economic recession may in fact *generate* specific types of demand attractive for foreign labour.[21]

In other words, after the "recruitment stop" in most European countries, particularly after the early 1980s, the share of foreigners and immigrants has increased in the total population (OECD 1995). Furthermore, the composition of the group has changed in favour of family members of original migrants, asylum seekers and an indistinct group of "illegals" – huge, yet impossible to estimate accurately.[22]

The possibilities of entry as an asylum seeker, have made the "stop" policies less effective, in turn obscuring the traditional distinction between the "economic" migrant and the "political" migrant (refugee). Information flows to areas that are "producing" asylum seekers tell that four out of five of these migrants manage to stay in Europe even though they

---

21. This last point was stressed by Jorge Bustamente during the OECD conference on Migration and International Cooperation: Challenges for the OECD Countries, in Madrid, 29–31 March 1993.
22. According to recent OECD figures, arrivals of immigrants seeking work or to rejoin their families predominate in most European OECD countries, and the numbers are higher in absolute terms than arrivals of asylum seekers, except in Sweden (OECD Observer 1992).

Table 2. Immigration (gross) to Western European countries

	1985	1986	1987	1988	1989	1990	1991	1992
Regular immigration of foreigners	700,000	750,000	800,000	950,000	1,150,000	1,200,000	1,300,000	1,300,000
Asylum-seekers	170,000	200,000	180,000	220,000	310,000	430,000	550,000	690,000
Ex-Yugoslavs offered TPS outside asylum procedures								350,000
Ex-nationals having a constitutional right to immigrate	100,000	100,000	150,000	300,000	800,000	450,000	300,000	300,000
Illegal entrants	50,000	50,000	50,000	100,000	100,000	200,000	300,000	400,000
Total	1,020,000	1,100,000	1,180,000	1,570,000	2,360,000	2,280,000	2,450,000	3,040,000

Source: Widgren 1993

have been refused status as refugees. Legal entrants who have overstayed now constitute the bulk of illegal immigrants in most European countries (Salt 1989). Although this distinction has been complicated from the outset, the fairly liberal policies of the Western countries with respect to asylum seekers have become a "pull" factor, which in turn has led the main receiving countries to revise their policies towards this category.

The point here is that the different streams of migrants are connected, and influence the actions and movements of one another. After the door was closed for *labour* migrants in the early 1970s, the only *legal* entry was through the asylum path and arrangements for family reunion. Having minute odds of succeeding through legal recruitment channels, foreign labour-seekers from "peaceful" countries in the South entered by means of unofficial channels. Presumed control of one gateway may consequently divert the flow into a new track.

In the following the immigration situation in Western Europe, up to the 1990s and the establishment of the European Union, will be spelled out in greater detail.

Chapter 3

The European Migration Pattern. Movements from the East and South[23]

According to John Salt (1992), we may trace four major trends in the European immigration scene since the mid-1980s. Firstly, there has been a rise in existing immigration flows, including labour migration. Secondly, there is the significant upsurge in the numbers of asylum seekers and refugees. This tendency, in existence since the beginning of the decade, underwent a marked acceleration by the end of the 1980s. Most of the claimants have been spontaneous, not part of re-settlement schemes or quota systems. Thirdly, a basically new flow of migrants has started entering the Southern European countries at the Mediterranean rim. This flow originates mainly in (Northern) Africa, and has predominately been illegal. Through this new tendency, the Southern European countries have turned from countries of emigration to countries of immigration. Fourthly, since 1989 the flows from the East have grown substantially.

In the following we will deal firstly with the fourth tendency, followed by the remaining three later in the chapter.

---

23. I will in this report use the term "Eastern Europe" or "the East" to apply to both Central and East European countries (Bulgaria, Romania, Albania, former Yugoslavia, former Czechoslovakia, Hungary, Poland, and partly the former Soviet Union. Accordingly, I will use the term "Western Europe" (unless otherwise specified) for all countries in the Western part of the continent, including the Southern and Northern European countries. By contrast, "the South" will be used as a collective concept for actual and potential sender-countries in the Third World in terms of immigration to Europe.

Migration from the East

The dramatic changes of 1989 have already altered the existing migration patterns on the European continent. The transformation, started through the liberalization process in the East followed by an improved East–West political climate, triggered off marked emigration pressures. The migration wave itself reinforced the process already in motion, and was to prove the immediate reason for the fall of the Berlin Wall in November 1989. With this major barrier gone, continued and intensified migration flows (partly encouraged by automatic citizenship in West Germany for ethnic Germans) contributed further to stepping up the unification process in Germany. In the course of 1989, 1.3 million people left their home area in the East (Council of Europe 1990).

In 1990, 197,000 Germans from DDR and 397,000 ethnic Germans from Eastern Europe came to West Germany. Since 1991, the year of German unification, migration from former DDR per definition stopped being registered as transnational migration, and consequently disappeared from the statistics of border-crossing individuals. The number of ethnic Germans from Eastern Europe was reduced to slightly more than half the size of 1990 in both 1991 and 1992 (220,000 people a year) (Fijalkowski 1993). Nevertheless, this trek to the

Table 3. Ethnic Germans migrating to Germany,* 1988–91 (thousands)

Source country	1988	1989	1990	1991	Total
Soviet Union	47	98	148	147	440
Poland	140	250	134	40	524
Romania	13	23	111	32	179
Total	203	377	397	222	1199

* Up to 1990, figures are for the Federal Republic of Germany; thereafter unified Germany.
Source: Bade 1993, referred in Stalker 1994

West represents one of the major migration waves in recent times.

The dismantling of the Wall has confronted the West with a series of dilemmas. The right to *emigrate* has been highly valued in the Western liberal and humanistic tradition, and has for long been a point of major criticism towards the East. The sudden and overwhelming achievement of this claim has meant that new barriers have been raised – from the West.

In the following the development and the apparent tendencies in the migration pattern East–West since 1989, on the basis of historical experiences, will be discussed.

Emigration from the East 1945–1989

All the East European countries have to varying degrees been *emigration* countries. Since the exit possibility was reduced after the Second World War, fewest people have left the former Soviet Union, followed by Bulgaria and Romania. Former Yugoslavia and Poland have had the strongest emigration together with the former DDR (Chesnais 1990).

Of all countries from the "Eastern Bloc", out-migration from the former Soviet Union has been the strongest and most efficiently controlled. Disregarding the popular movements as a result of changed borders after the war, only 500,000 people are registered as having left the Soviet Union during the period 1946–85 (Chesnais 1991).

Out-migration from former Czechoslovakia has by and large been limited to Germans from Sudetenland in 1946 (about 1.5 million) and refugee flows after the Soviet invasion in 1968 (when approximately 200,000 people left). Likewise, approximately 200,000 people left Hungary after the insurrection in 1956. Otherwise, only very few have left Hungary after the war.

For various reasons, significant groups have left both Poland and Yugoslavia since 1945. Both countries have been subject to major political transformations of their territories, and have historically experienced large-scale migrations. Due

Table 4. Inflow of migrants into Germany, 1950–1991

Thousands

	Ten-year average annual inflow				Annual inflow							
	1950–59	1960–69	1970–79	1980–89	1984	1985	1986	1987	1988	1989	1990	1991
Ethnic Germans from: Central and Eastern Europe (excluding Eastern Germany)	44.0	22.1	35.5	100.4	36.5	39.0	42.8	78.5	202.7	377.1	397.1	222.0
of which:												
Poland	29.2	11.1	20.3	51.6	17.5	22.1	27.2	48.4	140.2	250.3	133.9	40.1
Former USSR	1.4	0.9	5.7	22.6	0.9	0.5	0.8	14.5	47.6	98.1	148.0	147.3
Romania	–	1.6	7.1	22.6	16.6	14.9	13.1	14.0	12.9	23.4	111.2	32.2
Eastern Germany	220.3	61.8	14.9	58.5	41.0	24.9	26.2	19.0	39.8	343.9	381.3	–
Asylum seekers	–	–	15.6	77.6	35.3	73.8	99.7	57.4	103.1	121.3	193.1	256.1
Foreign migrants (net inflows)	–	–	–	3.3	–249.2	–42.3	30.9	80.9	186.4	211.2	182.5	157.8

Source: Ministry of the Interior, referred in OECD (SOPEMI) Annual Report 1993

to this situation, popular roots locally might be somewhat weaker than is the case for many other East Europeans. The Communist regime in Poland tried to *reduce* out-migration, but was never in a position to control it fully. In former Yugoslavia on the other hand, the government systematically encouraged parts of the population to seek employment in the West.

There is today great variation in demographic structure and size among the East European countries. The sharpest contrast is found between Hungary and former Czechoslovakia on the one hand and Poland and Romania on the other. While Hungary and former Czechoslovakia have had a very low population increase, Poland and Romania represent nearly 2/3 of the total population (96 million) in the five mentioned Eastern European countries, and they also represent the strongest increase rate (Chesnais 1990).

From the early 1970s till the mid-1980s, the total out-migration from the former Warsaw Pact countries (about 400 million people altogether), amounted to approximately 100,000 per year. Half of these were German immigrants to former West Germany: "Übersiedler" – refugees from former East Germany, and "Aussiedler" – refugees from another Eastern country (Chesnais 1991).

Immigration to Western Europe from the former Eastern Bloc has consequently been limited during the period after the Second World War, if we leave out the period immediately after the end of the war before the blocs were established. The marked turning point came in 1989.

Migration after 1989

After the events of 1989 both short-term migration (tourism, seasonal labour etc.), and more lasting emigration have flourished. Short-term migration has primarily affected Germany and Austria, although the Nordic countries and Western Europe in general have experienced this to some degree. Polish nationals have figured most frequently in this short-term traffic, to the extent that parts of the informal sector in many

Western European countries today are popularly labelled "Polish markets" (Hönekopp 1991). In Scandinavia, the Polish migrants have by and large left the country after their three months' legal stay. On the Continent the picture is more complex. Austria introduced a visa requirement for Polish nationals in August 1990, after a marked growth in Polish tourists who overstayed their legal period (OECD 1991). On the other hand, the bilateral agreements between the Schengen countries (see Chapter 4) and Poland of 1991, abolished visa requirements for Poles wanting to go to the Schengen countries.[24]

Immigration from Eastern Europe after 1989 has so far basically followed the same ethnic and geographical pattern as before. Population groups with connections through the (recent or distant) past or through ethnic origin are heading westward to regions where they in one way or another feel they "belong". This concerns, e.g. (former) East Germans, Poles, and Czechs moving to (former) West Germany; Hungarians and other Czechs to Austria; and Bulgarians and Romanians to Turkey and Hungary respectively (OECD 1991). There have also been reinforcements of already established "routes", like that from Poland to France; from Russia, Hungary, and Poland to Canada/USA; from Russia to Israel, and to some extent to Finland and the other Nordic countries.

Immigration from the East has, however, changed character in the sense that there is no automatic or easy access to political asylum anymore.[25] Thus, the new waves from the East represent a blurred category in the sense that it is not regular labour migration nor moves induced primarily by fear of per-

---

24. Sweden and Norway also abolished visa requirements for Polish nationals in 1991.
25. *Applications* for asylum from the East are still significant, however. Even after the new and more restrictive asylum law was past in Germany in July 1993, Romanian asylum-seekers still represent the largest contingent: 73,717 in 1993, 22.8% of the total number. Other notable groups are Bulgarians (22,547), Bosnians (21,240) and Turks (19,104) (*Migration News Sheet*, February 1994).

Table 5. Foreign resident nationals from Central and Eastern Europe in some European OECD countries as of 31 December 1991

	Belgium	Finland (1992)	France (1990)	Germany	Sweden	Switzerland
			Number (1, 000)			
Bulgaria	–	0.3	0.8	32.6	–	0.6
Former CSFR	0.5	0.2	2.0	46.7	–	5.6
Hungary	0.7	0.4	2.9	56.4	3.3	4.5
Poland	4.8	0.7	46.3	271.2	16.1	5.2
Romania	–	0.3	5.7	92.1	5.5	2.6
Former USSR	0.9	15.2	4.3	–	–	0.8
Total foreigners	922.5	40.8	3596.6	5882.3	493.8	1163.2
			Share in the total foreign population (%)			
Bulgaria	–	0.7	–	0.6	–	0.1
Former CSFR	0.1	0.4	0.1	0.9	–	0.5
Hungary	0.1	0.9	0.1	1.1	0.7	0.4
Poland	0.5	1.7	1.3	5.2	3.3	0.5
Romania	–	0.7	0.2	1.8	1.1	0.2
Former USSR	0.1	37.2	0.1	–	0.1	–
Total foreigners	100.0	100.0	100.0	100.0	100.0	100.0

Sources: Population registers and, for France, population censuses, referred in OECD (SOPEMI) Annual Report 1993

secution. A significant number of the current asylum seekers in Germany come from the areas from which migrant workers used to come before the recruitment stop of the 1970s: former Yugoslavia and Romania.

Migration has not only increased *East–West* in Europe. The new democracies in the East – Hungary, the Czech and Slovak Republics, and Poland – have also become receiving countries. Immigration in this context basically involves other neighbouring countries where the situation is worse (Romania, Bul-

Table 6. Available information on immigration and emigration flows, 1988–1991, Hungary

Year	Asylum seekers	Immigration	Return migration	Emigration Legal	Emigration Illegal
1988	13 173	5 774	515	1 358	3 506
1989	17 448	10 180	901	1 267	–
1990	18 283	17 129	2 041	1 285	–
1991	54 693	20 500	2 235	778	–

Source: Ministry of the Interior, referred in OECD (SOPEMI) Annual Report 1993

Table 7. Inflow of asylum seekers in Hungary, 1988–1992

Year	Registered asylum seekers	Country of origin	Share in total (%)
1988	13 173	Romania	99.0
1989	17 448	Romania	98.0
1990	18 283	Romania	95.0
		Former USSR	2.0
1991	54 693	Former Yugoslavia	87.0
		Romania	10.0
1992 (January to July)	9 297	Former Yugoslavia	91.0
		Romania	5.1

Source: Ministry of the Interior, referred in OECD (SOPEMI) Annual Report 1993

garia, and republics from the former Soviet Union) as well as parts of the developing world.[26] For instance, Hungary has been receiving immigrants who are Arabs, Romanians, and former Soviet citizens.

Besides, in 1992 Hungary and Poland faced a sharp increase in the number of attempted illegal border crossings

26. Not only has East–East *migration* increased; short-term visits, ostensibly for tourist purposes, have shown a market increase. Poland received 7 million tourists from the former Soviet Union in 1991. There are indications that some of these movements are for commercial purposes (Commission 1994).

(Commission 1994). Both Poland and Hungary have recently become stepping stones to the West for some immigrant groups. A new "pecking order" has emerged: Poland has introduced a visa requirement for Romanians, while thousands of Poles are moving West – primarily to Germany. Even though emigration from East Europe has increased significantly since 1989, the registered figures in the West are lower than expected (see, e.g. OECD 1991 and Hönekopp 1991). What then, is the likely future of migration patterns East–West? Which dimensions of East European societies can give us an indication of the future potential?

Emigration potential in the East

If we view the former Eastern Bloc as a whole, we may differentiate two main types of motivation behind a move westward, although the demarcation is not always very clear: 1) Ethnically/politically motivated and; 2) economically motivated migration.

In the former Soviet Union we find what Chesnais (1991) labels "a unique combination of 'push-factors'": Economic backwardness, lack of functioning democracy, nationalistic uprisings and inter-ethnic conflicts. Moreover, a significant number of the inhabitants are resourceful in terms of education and other qualifications for which they are not sufficiently rewarded at home at present. Theoretically, there should consequently be a notable emigration potential in the former Soviet Union.

However, calculations over likely rates of emigration from the former Soviet Union vary considerably. For the period 1991–93, Soviet emigration was projected at between 3 and 20 million (Salt 1992); a former Soviet government secretary made in 1990 a far-reaching estimate at 15–45 million (*Information* 9 May 1990); and the French Demographic Institute INED forecasts 1.5 million *annually* for some years to come (*Information* 29–30 December 1990). The discrepancies in figures reflect the uncertainties attached to the issue. Many strategic factors are unknown, and besides, from the "sender" side, *political* messages may be hidden in the calculations. From various sources it has been suggested that speculative figures are presented so as to get more aid from the West for the sender economies (see, e. g. Chesnais 1991; Stölting 1991). So far the mass exit from the former Soviet Union has been long in coming.

Ethnicity

As to the ethnic minorities, certain groups would seem to have a higher propensity to migrate than others. Prime among these are the minorities with a profound ethnic consciousness and who have already been emigrating (Salt 1992). Up till the collapse of the Soviet Union, emigration from the empire involved primarily three ethnic groups, Germans, Jews, and Armenians. Together, these constituted 95 per cent of all emigration from the USSR (Chesnais 1991). A second group of potential migrants includes those who have their ancestry in neighbouring nationalities, the Poles being the largest of these (approximately one million). Bulgarians, Finns, and Turks are also found in this group. A third category consists of Westernized minorities, the largest group being Balts (5.5 million). This group may number some 14 million people altogether – with higher education, knowledge of foreign languages and other valuable skills (Salt 1992).

It has been calculated that more than 3 million ethnic Germans outside the borders of Germany can claim their rights as "Aussiedlers". A fairly high number of these are expected to move to Germany in the near future. 1.5 million remaining Jews – basically in Russia – are also expected to emigrate either to Israel or to the USA. More significantly, Armenians are expected to constitute a major movement out of their current territories, which belong to the most conflict-ridden areas of the former empire: Armenia, Azerbaijan, and Georgia. Armenians have long traditions of migration, today making up large immigrant communities in both France (about

300,000) and the USA (about 500,000). Experts calculate that the new streams of Armenians will follow basically the same paths as before (see Chesnais 1991; Okolski 1990). In total, there are some 15 minorities in the former Soviet Union which, according to Chesnais, possess a strong ethnic consciousness and a feeling of belonging to some place outside their current home country. These groups constitute a population of about 20 million altogether, which have not been well integrated into the Soviet Union nor in their respective republics (*Information* 29–30 December 1990).

However, even though these people may have stronger connections outside their country than the rest of the population, it is uncertain how many would actually want to emigrate. Several opinion polls have been undertaken in the former Soviet Union and the rest of Eastern Europe to estimate the potential. According to a survey of 3,000 Soviet citizens in 1990, 16 per cent wanted to emigrate: this equals 46 million people (Chesnais 1991). Predictions based on such surveys are highly uncertain, however. There is a big difference between responding positively to theoretical questions, and actually moving.[27]

Economy

Differences in standard of living play an important role for the economically motivated potential in Eastern Europe. This difference was in 1988 illustrated the following way: To buy one kilo of meat one had to work 2–5 times longer in the East than, e.g. in former West Germany. To buy a colour TV 4–13 times longer; a car 2–9 times longer (Okolski 1990). Purchasing power has been further drastically reduced since 1988 in several of the Eastern countries in question.

---

27. Another survey undertaken by the Norwegian research institute FAFO on the Kola Peninsula reveals a different picture: Only 3 per cent of the population expressed any wish to emigrate (*Aftenposten* 2 June 1993).

Table 8. Selected basic indicators of the economic situation in 1992

Country	GNP growth rate	Inflation rate (consumer price)	Unemployment rate
Bulgaria	−21.0	179.4	16.4
Former CSFR	−7.0	10.7	5.4
Hungary	−5.0	23.0	14.0
Poland	+0.5	43.0	14.3
Romania	−15.4	210.4	8.2

Sources: OECD, Short-Term Economic Indicators, Central and Eastern Europe. 2/1993. Employment Observer, Commission of the European Communities. Referred in OECD (SOPEMI) Annual Report 1993

Access to labour is another central factor. Economists and demographers at INED point to the fact that up till 1995, some 44 million people in the former Soviet Union, 6 million Poles, and 4 million Romanians will be between 15 and 25 years of age. Of these, 50 per cent are calculated to be unemployed or strongly underemployed, i.e. 40 million in the former Soviet Union and 5 million in Poland.[28]

Even though differences both in standard of living, access to labour and political security/liberty may be considerable between the respective countries of the East and West, these are not alone sufficient reasons for thousands of people to break up and leave their homes. Differences between Western Europe and regions in the Third World are much greater, without there having been established a "migration bridge" for that reason. In judging the possible/likely future patterns of migration between East Europe/former USSR and West Europe, we need to consider a broader context.

---

28. Quoted in *Information* 29–30 December 1990.

What will influence the migration pattern from the East?

Up till 1989, refugees dominated the immigration picture from the East. Asylum seekers from countries which have lagged behind in the democratization process still represent a part of the westward flow. In addition, a great many people come in search of work, legally or illegally. This pattern will most likely continue in the future, the internal composition of the migration streams being dependent on conditions in the sender countries, in the receiver countries and on the linkages in between.

The most important factors which may influence the patterns of future East–West migration in Europe can for reasons of clarity be divided into three groups. 1) "push factors": economic ethnic/political and demographic "ejection mechanisms" in sender societies; 2) "pull factors", or the attractions in the receiver countries: economic and social conditions (welfare provisions), labour market parameters, political freedom and possible familiar/cultural bonds; 3) policies in the East and the West (nation-state and/or EU level), respectively, which stimulate or hamper migration.

An interplay of these three clusters of factors will decide the scale, type and direction as to future migration. I will in the following briefly discuss each cluster in relation to possible future East–West migration.

"Push factors"

Demography
Experts widely agree that demographic conditions will not be the prime factor in explaining East–West migration. Demographic variables rarely constitute causal factors in themselves; besides, the population increase in the Eastern part of Europe is not on a scale likely to foster migration pressure. Romania might represent an exception in this respect, as could the former USSR. Within the territory of the former Soviet Un-

ion, however, there is great demographic variation. During the last ten years, the Soviet population has on average grown with 0.4 per cent in Belorussia, 0.7 per cent in Russia, 1.3 in Kazakhstan and 2.9 in Uzbekistan. Furthermore, a comparison between East and West Europe concerning age groups (below 15 years; 15–64 years; and 65 and above) reveals a relatively parallel development in demographic composition (Hönekopp 1991).

Ethnic/political factors
Ethnic/political factors are far more complex and uncertain. As a main tendency, we might expect politically motivated migration to diminish with increasing democratization. Paradoxically, the *possibilities* of migrating after the liberalization of exit controls might have devalued the attraction: One of the formerly most important reasons for wanting to leave has been removed. On the other hand, impatience with the slow progress of the liberalization/democratization process may provoke streams of more mobile population groups, such as youth with educational resources.[29]

Liberalization has also brought out into the open ethnic tensions and conflicts that for various reasons did not materialize under the repressive regimes during the Cold War. Societies on the territory of the former USSR have shown themselves highly vulnerable and volatile as to national/ethnic tensions. This may revitalize the *political* motivation for emigrating, although several of these conflicts might generate "East–East" migration rather than East–West, at least in the first round.

Former Yugoslavia is, in this context, the area of ethnic conflict with strongest impact on Western Europe at present. In terms of movements of people, the consequences of the conflict have affected practically all the Western European coun-

---

29. Studies from Poland in the 1980s reveal that almost complete cohorts of graduates left the country. "Brain-drain" is now considered a notable problem also in Romania and Bulgaria. A Survey among students in Croatia in 1991 disclosed that the majority wanted to emigrate, after having finished higher education (*Ny i Sverige*, 4/91).

tries.[30] Approximately four million people from former Yugo-slavia are today refugees – whether internally in the area which used to be Yugoslavia, in a neighbouring country, or further afield (Flyktningerådet 1994). The crisis has provoked basic discussions on refugee policies in relation to war situations, and has led the most affected countries to revise their asylum policies. This formidable "push" induced by a violent political/ethnic conflict has alerted the Western nations to refugee potentials in the former Eastern Bloc.

Economic factors

The most significant future "push factor" in the whole of the former Warsaw Pact area is nevertheless economic development in the wake of the reform process. In this respect there are different preconditions for optimism in the various countries.

The transformation to market economy implies that more people will become unemployed or "underemployed". This situation becomes further aggravated by the fact that social security arrangements are by far capable of meeting the needs (Hönekopp 1991). In the short run, there has already been a further deterioration of conditions, in terms of lower real wages and poor access to goods, whether through real deficiencies or through hyperinflation.

Conditions in the agricultural sector will play a major role in terms of employment and access to goods. In all the Eastern countries, with the exception of the former Czechoslovakia, the proportion of the population employed in agriculture is around 20 per cent (Bulgaria, Hungary, and the former USSR) and 30 per cent (Poland, Romania, and former Yugoslavia).

---

30. As usual, some countries are more strongly affected than others. Six Western European states have now received more than 90% of the refugees from Bosnia: Germany, Sweden, Denmark, Norway, Switzerland, and Austria (*Information*, 30/11 1993). Germany has accepted more Bosnian refugees than the other five taken together: as of January 1994, Germany had received 300,000 Bosnians, a figure that is rising by approximately 6,000 per month (*Migration News Sheet*, January 1994).

Any attempt to make the (by and large) low-productive farms more efficient would lead to redundant labour, not easily absorbed in other fields of production – at least not in the short run (Okolski 1990). The Eastern European countries are here facing a major dilemma.

Much will depend on how economic, political, and social changes will interplay and relate to popular expectations. How quickly societies are captured by a positive dynamics,[31] which at least can give hope that conditions will improve "in not too long", will decide whether people are willing to tolerate a demanding transitional period. People's motivation for mentally investing in a difficult period will be decisive – not only for the capability to transform society, but also for the ability to retain valuable labour power. Among the authorities in the East, there is as much concern about mass emigration as the Westerners fear mass immigration (*Berlingske Tidende*, 16 June 1991). Loss of their Western-oriented, well-educated minorities could be highly unfortunate for the Eastern countries today. About one in six Polish emigrants during the period 1983–87 had higher education, and the medical and engineering professions were most severely affected (Salt 1992). If the Eastern countries were to be drained of strategic labour during the highly vulnerable period of transition, this could easily lead to a major setback in economic and social development, which again would serve to maintain emigration. The loss of skills and commitment of the young and more active parts of the work force would be significant when new enterprises and structures are to be developed.[32] Hungary presents an interesting case in this context. The country was the first in the East to open its borders, without experiencing any mass exodus. Even before the borders were opened, the state had apparently come quite far in the restructuring process which the

---

31. The degree of recovery varies significantly. For the time being (late 1994), the Czech and the Polish republics are experiencing promising economic growth.
32. So far sufficient data is lacking about the scale and composition of the emigration flow to be able to evaluate these effects in detail (see OECD 1992).

other countries are now facing. This fact may prove to be an important difference.

Economists believe that, in the short and medium term, the East–West income gap will *widen* (Hönekopp 1991). This will make demands on people's patience in the East, particularly now that the information flow from the West has grown and the Western way of life has by no means lost its attraction.

"Pull factors"

The "pull forces" in the West have to a certain extent changed character with the liberalization of the Eastern regions. The relative importance of democratic liberties as an attraction in the West has been reduced apace with the changes in the East. At the same time, the liberty to leave has activated other "pull forces" primarily economic, but also ethnic/cultural and social ones.

Proximity and network

Within migration research factors like cultural and geographic proximity are seen as central to explanations of why specific migration "bridges" are established. Eastern Europe and parts of the former USSR fulfil both criteria in relation to Western Europe. Despite the very restrictive emigration regulations, many places in the East, networks between emigrants, and "remainers" were established across the East–West divide. In a 1984 study in Poland, two-thirds of the respondents said that assistance from relatives abroad was of central importance concerning their decision to visit the country in question and subsequently find a job and settle. Of the two million Poles who have settled in Western Europe, the great majority have chosen Germany[33] (Okolski 1990).

With the increased possibilities of moving westward, this self-reinforcing network effect may have even stronger impact

---

33. There is also a sizable group in France.

than before. The more people who move, the more information flows back to the areas of origin, and new potential migrants may feel safer that if they should choose to go, there will be people to receive them and assist in the process of establishment. Besides, general access to information from the West has grown with liberalization. This "information effect" might, however, strike both ways, if conditions on the receiving end take an unfavourable turn, like economic recession or hostility towards foreigners. It nevertheless appears that when there is a marked *difference* in standard of living between the sending and receiving areas, potential migrants will listen more to specific examples to the effect that "so and so has found work and is doing well in Paris" than macro-descriptions of conditions at large. Hearing enough examples of success, the potential migrant may decide to take the chance.

The regular labour market[34]
The development in the labour market in Western Europe will play an important role when it comes to the strength of the "pull forces" in the near future. Calculations of labour demand in the European market are, however, often contradictory. Gradually, demographic development has been granted more attention in the West. Since 1972 there have been six million more deaths than births in the area of unified Germany (Chesnais 1990). This indicates an age composition with elderly as a disproportionally large group in the years to come, which would threaten value production and reproduction in society. Labour-force projections indicate that employment in the EU countries will rise more rapidly than labour-force growth by the year 2000. A recent estimate foresees a contraction of the European Community's labour force by 5.5 per cent – from 145 million in 1990 to 137 million over the next three decades (Ghosh 1992).

Simultaneously, there exists some optimism in the Euro-

---

34. The labour market dimension will be discussed in more depth in Chapter 7.

pean Community as to the employment effect of the Internal Market. It is believed that cost reductions and efficient measures attached to the establishment of the Union will expand employment considerably. The combination of these two factors – prospective shortages in the labour market and the growth in job creation – could suggest a more liberal attitude towards immigration. The authorities in West European countries have, however, been reluctant to enter into such a discussion. There is a large labour potential in terms of unemployed, non-employed or "under"-employed women and an already considerable degree of unemployment throughout the Community. This contradictory picture of the European labour market can furthermore be supplemented by general "mismatch" problems: lack of correspondence between demand and supply. The kind of labour which dominates the supply side through immigration does not necessarily harmonize with current deficiencies in the labour market.

The actual demand in the Western labour market, and the limited flexibility/geographic mobility of the native work force, have led employers in some places in Europe to pressure the authorities to relax restrictions on foreign labour. In Germany this has meant a revival of a "guestworker" system in a new form: as contract workers. This policy came as a response to claims, particularly from representatives of the agricultural sector, who were dissatisfied with the immigration policy contained in the recruitment stop of 1973. The German authorities had basically adhered to the "stop" policy up till the events of 1989; then with the openings eastward, it was decided to let in workers from the CCE countries (Rudolph and Hübner 1993). This is a question of *temporary* contracts of 12–18 months duration, established with workers from neighbouring countries (Poland, Hungary, Russia, Romania, Bulgaria, and the former Czechoslovakia). These contracts represent either "border labour" ("Grense-Arbeit"), where the workers commute from their own country on a daily or weekly basis, or quotas of specific types of labour. These contract workers have no rights to social insurance benefits, and they are not entitled to bring any family members with them. Furthermore, this kind of contract labour receives remarkably low wages, since the employers can pay "local salaries" (market price). As distinct from the former "guest workers", these contract workers are engaged by contractors in the sender country and not by German companies. The number of such contract workers was in 1992 calculated to be around 60,000 per month on average (Faist 1994). Through this contract labour system the German authorities may regain some of the flexibility from the period of the "guest-worker" system, while at the same time intentionally avoiding the settlement aspect from the 1960s and 1970s. Italy, Spain, France, and Luxembourg are currently embarking on similar temporary recruitment systems (Commission 1993).[35]

The unofficial labour market
On top of this new regular (although limited) opening in the West European labour market for foreigners, there exists a *de facto* demand for foreign (cheap) labour in the irregular parts of the market. Illegal migration is not a new phenomenon in Europe, and it has to be assessed in light of the restrictive policies on foreign labour, as indicated earlier. After the "immigration stop" in the 1970s, and, not the least, the events of 1989, this kind of labour has, however, received more public attention along with rising figures and the related social/political problems. The changes in the East–West relations and the severe problems affecting the former Eastern Bloc have enlarged the illegal contingent in Western Europe, in Germany in particular.[36] German authorities believe that for

---

35. Another, rather peculiar, quota arrangement recently appeared in one of the member countries: The British government announced in December 1989 that a quota of 50,000 Hong Kong ethnic Chinese would be allowed into the country provided each was individually in possession of more than £150,000, and intended to use the money as capital to employ British citizens (King 1992).
36. Calculations for 1981–88 indicate that illegal immigration to Germany from Poland exceeded those moving officially by 70% (Okolski 1991).

every person caught trying to cross the border illegally, three others succeed in avoiding arrest (*Migration News Sheet*, March 1994). The rising number of illegals in Western Europe has also exposed the deficiencies of existing policies and mechanisms to deal with transformations in the international migration systems, at the same time as it is a result of the same deficiencies.

Another notable tendency in the 1980s and 1990s is the connection between asylum seekers and illegal immigration in both Eastern and Western Europe. In the past, illegal immigration was predominantly linked to *labour* movements, but now the issue is increasingly coupled with the complicated question of political asylum (see Ghosh 1992). The significant rise in total numbers of asylum seekers entering Western Europe (from 170,000 in 1985 to 690,000 in 1992 [Widgren 1993]), has affected illegal immigration in the sense that many of the asylum seekers whose applications are rejected do find jobs in the shadow market, and consequently stay on irregularly. Countries in Eastern Europe, like Poland, former Czechoslovakia, and Hungary, are also affected by this unclear status and uncertain prospects as asylum seekers/refugees residing on their territory (Ghosh 1992).[37]

Yet another dimension adds to the untidy picture of irregular immigration to Europe. With tourism growing into a major industry, and with the liberalization of travelling possibilities in the Eastern regions, *legal* entry through tourist visas has become an avenue for illegal employment and extended stays.

The existence of a black economy relying on cheap labour contributes significantly to the "pull" mechanisms in Western Europe. It seems that irregular migration (more so than regular migration) functions in a self-perpetuating way, through the use of networks and social/kinship contacts at both ends

---

37. These countries have been affected by the recently introduced "first country" principle (Dublin Convention – see Chapter 4), where safe-transit countries are considered the proper place to submit an asylum application.

(Ghosh 1992).[38] On the other hand, the variation in structure of the labour market (size and quality of the black market, among other factors), is one of the complicating factors in the harmonization process at the European level.

The political level

It is evident that the *policies* being developed – both in the East and in the West – will influence the magnitude of migration, the type of migrants and the direction in which they move. Policies are important as a structural framework, although the "market forces of migration" have their own momentum, and although control in terms of laws and regulations has proved to be only necessary, not sufficient preconditions for managing migration.

Control policies at the receiving end are the major focus of this book. On the sending side, infrastructural aspects are central as to exit hindrances since emigration was liberalized. It costs a lot of time and money to leave these countries, or at least some of them. The processing period for visa applications in embassies becomes protracted as the queues grow; transport capacity is a problem, at least in certain areas; access to foreign currency represents a limitation, as does the exchange rate, etc. The rubel has seen repeated devaluations. A Russian tourist who wanted to visit Denmark in 1991 had to pay 5,500 rubles for 1,300 Danish Kroner, which at that time represented nearly two years salary for an average worker (*Information* 15 May 91). The surprisingly low extent of emigration from Russia since liberalization of the exit rules is partly explained by these factors.

Yet the most important premise as to future East–West migration is the question of how soon the East can achieve polit-

---

38. It seems that specific economic activities among immigrants can operate as a "pull" factor for further immigration, legal or illegal. Rinus Penninx uses the example of Turkish clothing workshops in Amsterdam, which employ an estimated 10,000 Turks, both legal and illegal (Amersfoort and Penninx 1994).

ical stability and economic progress. In this context political relations, followed by economic backing, are essential.

One result of the rapid disintegration of the Eastern Bloc after 1989 has been an accelerated rapprochement process between the East European states[39] and the Community. In public Western politicians have stressed the urgency of East–West integration in Europe, yet in practical terms this very process has been fraught with complications. Whereas economic *transfers* in terms of aid and loans have been generally non-controversial (although the volume has been disappointing to the Eastern states), access to Western markets has been the major stumbling block. Among the few competitive goods the East can offer, agricultural products predominate. Agriculture represents the sector which most rapidly and without extensive investments could furnish Eastern countries, particularly Poland, with the necessary capital to modernize other sectors of the economy. Yet with the excess production of many agricultural products, the EU is reluctant to open up its market to Eastern products. Particularly the French and German peasants have been militantly opposed to agricultural agreements with the East. Also other products have been controversial, like textiles, steel and coal. The association agreements between the EU and some of the Eastern states have thus far been less promising than envisaged. Although the association agreements have done little to create lasting structural preconditions for economic growth, they are of symbolic significance, and might even have an impact on the future migration pressure. Expectations might contribute psychologically to the creation of more stability, thereby stemming some of the potential drive to leave.

The new restrictive policy towards asylum seekers in the major receiving countries in Western Europe has to a certain

---

39. The Eastern countries vary in the way they are conceived by the EU states. Poland, Hungary, and particularly the Czech Republic are considered more promising as trade and investment partners than, e.g. Romania and the republics of the former Soviet Union (with the exception of Russia) (Giorgi et al. 1992).

degree been "successful" seen from the point of view of the authorities. The principle of lodging the application in the "first safe country" has, in effect, created a *cordon sanitaire* around the Western states. This fact, which detrimentally affects the former transit countries of the Eastern parts of Europe, has implied a significant reduction in the number of applications in the biggest receiving country in the whole of Europe – Germany.[40] There are, however, uncertainties as to whether this will be a lasting effect. Much depends on the agreement with the various "first safe countries", and on the "adjusted behaviour" of the asylum seekers. An increasing number of asylum seekers currently arrive in Germany without identity documents, hereby effectively hampering the newly introduced "quick process" of asylum applications.

Prospects of East–West migration

We have in this section looked into some central premises relevant to likely future migration to the EU area from Eastern Europe/former Soviet Union. This sending area is vast and culturally multifarious, which makes it difficult to forecast likely migration patterns. The situation in the former Warsaw Pact area is politically and economically unstable yielding a potential for both ethnically/politically motivated moves and regular labour migration. The former is likely to develop with increasing economic problems and social/ethnic tensions. However, it seems that such migration from the former USSR will *primarily* affect other countries in the region – as is, to a certain extent, already taking place (see OECD 1992). On the other hand, labour-related East–West migration may well continue and expand until the economic and social prospects in the sending areas improve. The prevailing phenomenon

---

40. In Scandinavia, where the number of Bosnian war refugees increased strongly in the first half of 1993, a visa requirement was introduced successively in the three countries. As acquiring visa under the prevailing conditions in the war zone is complicated, the number of applications was effectively reduced.

where people travel as tourists, but simultaneously search for work is likely to continue, likewise with seasonal/contract workers who overstay their legal period. So far, however, the mass exodus from the East envisaged by some, has not materialized.

Experts seem to believe that future streams from the East will basically follow existing routes, due to the network effect and historical traditions. This means that immigration from the East will primarily affect Germany, Austria, and, to a certain extent, France. New courses might, however, be established, depending on the strength of the pressures, and, of course, to what extent the receiving countries succeed in their control policies, and their (albeit reluctant) suggestions of "burden sharing".

Migration from the South

Whereas East–West migration made a sudden quantitative leap along with the events in 1989, there has been immigration from the South for many years, in varying forms and with altering areas of origin. Until the early 1970s, when the economic recession reduced labour demand in Western Europe, there existed basically two recruitment systems for foreign labour: the "guest-worker" system (primarily West Germany) and the "post-colonial" systems in the former colonial powers of Europe (most typically represented by France, the UK, and the Netherlands). Whereas the post-colonial powers recruited labour by utilising their historical connections to countries in the Third World, Germany "compensated" for its lack of such connections by establishing a systematic recruitment system through bilateral agreements (Portes and Böröcz 1989).

Concerning immigration from the South there are also well-trodden paths from the period before the mid-1970s. Most migrants came from the countries around the Mediterranean: Greece, Spain, Turkey, Portugal, Yugoslavia, and southern Italy. The composition of the migrant community in each re-

Figure 2. Inflows of permanent migrants to some OECD countries. Distribution by region of origin. In per cent

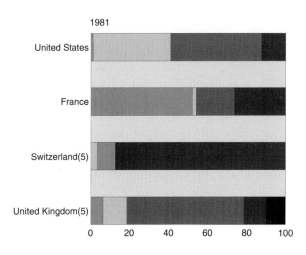

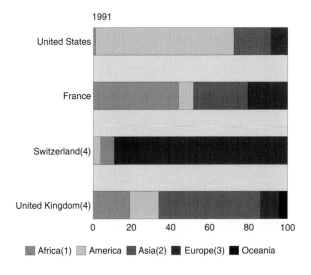

■ Africa(1) ▨ America ■ Asia(2) ■ Europe(3) ■ Oceania

1 Africa and Middle East for Canada.
2 Asia and Pacific for Canada. Including Turkey for all countries.
3 Including the former USSR.
4 Only the nationalities for which data were available are represented here.
Source: SOPEMI Annual Report 1993

ceiving country was however, varying. Greeks, Turks, and Yu-goslavs went to Germany; Algerians, Portuguese, Spaniards, Italians, and West Africans went to France; whereas the original influx to the UK and the Netherlands was dominated by the colonial bonds (India, Pakistan, British Caribbean to the UK; Indonesia, the other Dutch East-Asian colonies, and Surinam to the Netherlands). Belgian immigration mainly arrived from Spain, Morocco, Greece, and Turkey, whereas immigrants to Luxembourg came mainly from Spain and Portugal (Cohen 1987).

It is today evident that, apart from Germany, the main destination countries of illegal immigration to Europe are Greece, Italy, Spain, and Portugal. Changes in the economy of these former countries of *emigration* have expanded their demand for unskilled labour. Since the mid-1980s there has been an increase in the demand for labour in areas not attractive for the native population, notably the service sector. The general economic conditions have led to a thriving underground economy, with opportunities for illegal immigrants. Simultaneously, the rise in immigration in the Southern parts of Europe can partly be seen as a result of stricter regulations and tighter border controls in the Northern countries (Salt 1992).

In Western Europe there has been a tendency towards greater diversification of origins, with proportionally more immigrants coming from the Third World. Regional proximity being a determinant in migratory movements, the Mediterranean Southern rim represents one of the major sending regions. Yet areas further afield are also present in the streams to Europe: Cape Verde, Philippines, Eritrea, Somalia, Jordan, Egypt, Latin America, Gambia, Ghana, Guinea, Sri Lanka, etc. Out of 1,158,000 *registered* immigrants to Italy, Spain, Greece, and Portugal, about 25 per cent arrived from Third World countries. Including illegal immigrants, this figure is calculated to about 50 per cent (Salt 1992).

Changes in refugee migration

Up until the 1980s the refugee influx to Western Europe had remained small. Prior to the 1970s acute refugee flows from the Third World rarely affected the North, but moved primarily within the parts of the world where they originated.[41] West European governments could then channel money through the UN system and sometimes bilaterally, without being confronted with the problems within their own borders.

This picture changed during the 1970s with the crisis in Indo-China and the *coup d'état* in Chile. The subsequent flows of people made "jet refugee" a concept in Europe. However, in the 1970s the flows were not yet on a scale that really worried the receiving states. Only in the 1980s did the numbers of "jet refugees" become a major concern in Western Europe.

As we have seen, the "immigration stop" introduced in most Western European countries in the mid-1970s changed the composition of the inflow. Labour migration was replaced by refugees/asylum seekers, illegal migrants, and people qualifying under family reunion arrangements. According to statistical/political reports from the various EU countries, "*legal* arrivals have played only a small part over the last years in the real increase in the numbers of third country nationals resident in the EEC". The two major causes of this situation are said to be "abuses of the right of asylum" and "illegal immigration" (Commission 1992b:13). These two categories are increasingly linked in political statements and in the press. Of the two problems, the first is clearly most controversial. Whereas most people publicly would condemn illegal immigration and support most measures to eradicate the phenomenon, the question of asylum gives rise to heated debates, due to its humanitarian and symbolic implications. In the following the recent

---

41. Even though the general picture has changed somewhat, this is still the main tendency: 90% of the world's refugees originate in the Third World, and 90% of these again remain there, i.e. move to another Third World country (Loescher 1989).

history as to these two defined categories, and their possible interplay, will be discussed before going into the immigration potential from the South.

The number of asylum seekers has seen a steep increase during the late 1980s and early 1990s. Whereas the total number in 1985 was 170,000, this figure reached nearly 700,000 in 1992 (see Table 2, page 31). In the early 1990s, it seemed that after processing about 75 per cent of the applicants stayed on: 50 per cent legally and 25 per cent outside of the registers.

In the case of Germany (and Austria and Switzerland as well) the greatest share of asylum seekers has come (and still comes) from the former Eastern Bloc countries. Throughout Europe (Belgium, Sweden, Greece, Switzerland, Germany, France, Norway, the UK, and the Netherlands), a significant number also originate in the Third World. These figures are in many cases on the increase (Salt 1992). The movements in-

Figure 3. Asylum-seekers in Western Europe, 1980–90 (in thousands)

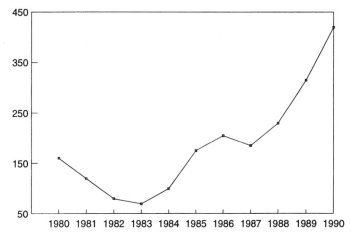

Ref.: Council of Europe, 1992
Source: Widgren 1993

volve a variety of nationalities, and the patterns are con-stantly changing. By and large, the major origins of these flows can be identified with areas of conflict, suppression, vio-lence, and outright war. Various sources persist, like Sri Lanka, Lebanon, Iran, Iraq, Turkey, and Somalia. Other countries have more or less faded out as sources of refugee streams, like Chile, Vietnam, and Korea. Some refugee connections can be explained by former colonial relations, like Zaire–Belgium. Others seem more coincidental from the outset, like Ghana–Norway and Somalia–Finland (Salt 1992).

Experience with asylum seeking varies substantially between the receiving states of Western Europe, and the in-flow has fluctuated rather sharply within the period in ques-tion. Generally speaking, numbers fell in the early years, par-ticularly in Germany. The picture then stabilized, with some variations, for a few years, to be followed by a steep rise in the late 1980s. Germany has again been a special case in this re-spect. The number of asylum seekers entering Germany rose from 193,000 in 1990 to 438,000 in 1992 (Commission 1993).[42] There are currently (1993/94) indications that this tendency is modified, at least temporarily. The latest reduction in numbers, compared to the peak year of 1992, is quite clearly a result of the new more restrictive Western policy to-wards asylum seekers. Since the entry into force of the new asylum law in Germany on 1 July 1993, the number of asy-lum seekers has been more than halved. The total number of entries in December 1993 was 14,033, the lowest monthly figure since March 1991 (*Migration News Sheet* February 1994).

The acceleration of asylum seeking from the latter part of the 1980s has confronted Europe with a new type of refugee

---

42. Along with this steep rise, however, the rate of recognition of refugee status has been declining from 16.2% in 1986 to 6.9% in 1991 and then 4.3% in 1992. It is estimated that 1.1 million persons (recognized political refugees and people accepted on humanitarian grounds) have arrived in Germany during the past few years (Commission 1993).

problem, where the traditional humanitarian approach has proven inadequate. The situation has caused great concern among the Western European governments, both as to the numbers, and the relatively unpredictable and unregulated character of the flows. Earlier, as we have seen, only very few "spontaneous" refugees from distant origins arrived in Europe. Refugees from the Third World basically meant quota refugees from UN controlled camps. With the new refugee flows, the vague distinction between "traditional" refugees and *ad hoc* refugees came into being. The former refers to those primarily accepted through the UN system, the latter without UN connections yet with claims of protection according to the UN Convention of 1951.

With this strong spontaneous influx there has come an accumulation of unprocessed cases and heavily overloaded administrations. Before the German reforms of 1993, it could take years to get a case processed. The costs (social benefits and administration)[43] have increased apace with the rising numbers, a fact increasingly used as an argument for further restrictions. Two other, related issues are added to the reasoning behind further restrictions: Increasingly hostile reactions against foreigners among the indigenous population, and the ensuing social tension; and consideration for UN refugees. It is assumed that such "quota refugees" are successively worse off in terms of stagnating (or reduced) quotas, since the refugee budget is absorbed by the new asylum seekers.

This general situation now constitutes a major threat to the institution of asylum. Various humanitarian organizations have pointed out the risk of the concept of asylum being undermined and the rights attached to it being questioned. People likely to benefit from the institution are being placed in a rigorous hierarchy.

---

43. Total expenditure on asylum administration in Europe increased 6 times during the 1980s (Loescher 1989).

Figure 4. Gross flows of immigrants and asylum seekers or refugees (origination both in the South and the East) in selected European OECD countries, 1980–91. In thousands

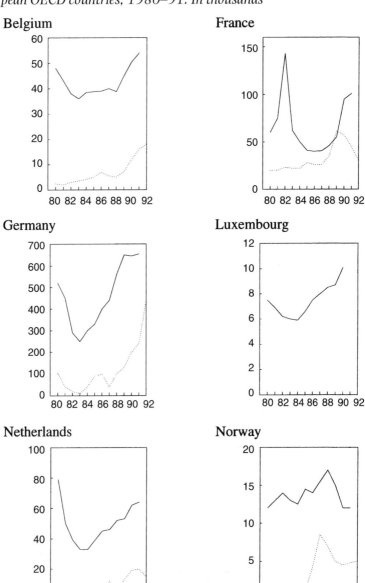

(Figure 4, continued)

Sweden

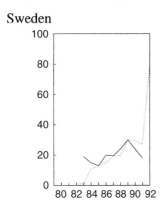

Switzerland

United Kingdom

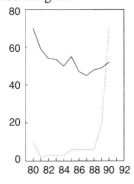

———— Entries of foreigners (excluding asylum seekers, seasonal and frontier
     workers)
·········· Entries of asylum seekers. Data for 1992 are provisional
Source: OECD (SOPEMI) Annual Report 1993

Illegal immigration from the South
A major limitation concerning studies of the black (unofficial)
labour market is, of course, lack of reliable data. To make the
phenomenon more visible, and thus easier to act upon, the authorities in Spain, Italy and France have several times in recent years introduced so-called "amnesties" or "regularizations", whereby the illegals may register and become "regular" without risking penalties.

The "amnesties" in Southern Europe have brought into the open various sides of the *labour* market that actually hire the illegal immigrants. Tougher economic conditions often tempt employers to hire illegally. The use of cheap foreign labour has become an important means for small and medium-sized firms to retain flexibility and lower production costs in a highly competitive situation. The service sector is typical in this respect, although other segments are also involved. In France, irregular labour is occupied basically in hotels, cafés, shops, in private households as well as in construction and the health sector, whereas in Spain and Italy such labour is concentrated in the tourist sector, private households, catering, as well as in agriculture. Furthermore, illegal migration in itself acts to foster economic activity. A Spanish police report recently revealed the existence of large networks exclusively dedicated to the lucrative business of clandestine immigration (*Migration News Sheet* March 1992).

Data from the "regularizations" reveal significant dimensions to the unregistered labour undertaken by illegal immigrants, and that illegals may stay in their "host" countries for years (OECD 1990). In Italy the "amnesty" of a few years back exposed over 100 foreign nationalities in the interstices of the labour market and commerce (ILO 1989). Regularized immigrants in Italy now account for more than one third of the residents from outside the European Union area (Commission 1992b). In Spain the number of foreigners in a regular situation increased from 85,000 in 1990 to 230,000 in 1992. Most of these appeared to be salaried workers (90 per cent), generally men (68 per cent) and more than half of them from Africa, most typically Morocco (40 per cent) (ibid.).[44]

The "amnesty" policy has brought into the open the dimen-

---

44. In 1991 the number of asylum requests fell in comparison with the previous year, a fact which is interpreted to mean that potential candidates "felt that the regularization procedure offered better chances of success" (Commission 1992b:10).

sion of the problem of illegal foreign labour,[45] and it has provided some thousands of foreign workers with better working and living conditions in the receiving countries. However, these "amnesties" also represent a double-edged sword for the authorities. Such regularizations are usually followed by a wave of secondary immigration of family members; moreover, they signal internationally that illegal entry may imply a legalized future.[46]

What will influence the migration pattern from the South?

Since there are few indications that *regular* immigration (as known from the period before the "immigration stop") from the South is on the EU agenda (see Chapter 4), and since the sending countries rarely can provide so-called "specified labour in demand" for the European countries, asylum seekers and illegal immigrants will most likely still dominate the influx.

In the following, the most important factors which may influence future migration patterns and possible immigration pressures on Europe from regions in the South will be assessed. As in the discussion on the trends from the East, emphasis will be placed on the interplay between "push" and "pull" forces in addition to the political conditions.

"Push factors"

Three central "push" factors or driving forces in the South can today be outlined, depending on the kind of migration in question: from the clearly political (the ideal-type refugee) to the more economic and social. In many developing countries the *demographic* factor has additionally come to the fore. Often a combination of these factors will be decisive. The dividing line

---

45. Although the people being regularized through such "amnesties" most likely represent the tip of the iceberg.
46. The question of illegal immigration will also be dealt with in Chapter 7.

between the political and economic reasons for migration is, as we have seen, difficult, and subject to continuous debates nationally and internationally.

Overpopulation and underdevelopment
In great parts of the Third World the economic and social situation has deteriorated gradually over the last 20 years, due to higher oil prices, high interest rates (after 1979/80), and a relative decline in prices on raw materials. This situation, combined with the marked population increase, has made living conditions worse, sometimes for the majority of the population. An increasing number of young and able people can not find work within their own regions; real wages have gone down, and in the rural areas land is often scarce.[47]

The juxtaposition of overpopulation and underdevelopment/slow development seems to affect rates of emigration: directed towards not too distant areas (e.g. rural–urban) in some contexts; and to areas further afield in others. It seems that the closer geographically a country with rapid population increase is located with respect to industrialized countries, the greater is the emigration pressure (OECD 1990).[48]

In (particularly Southern) Europe, immigration pressure has been strongest from North Africa – the Maghreb region. The countries of this region – Tunisia, Algeria, Morocco – have in recent years seen an accelerating population increase together with deteriorating terms of trade with the West. Political instability and ecological pressure[49] now add to this picture.

The combination of retarded population growth in the EU countries and continuing high rates of increase in the South

---

47. The steep population increase in the Third World is a major global problem of today, transcending by far the question of migration.
48. It needs to be stressed that the relations between development and emigration is highly complicated. It seems that development in terms of, e.g. better educational facilities for certain parts of the population may increase their inclination to migrate in the short run (see Teitelbaum 1991).
49. There are some forecasts that global warming will push the Sahara Desert closer to the Mediterranean, deteriorating the basis for agriculture and consequently food supply.

has made the Mediterranean area represent the sharpest demographic contrast in the world. In the 1960s the ratio of population growth between the countries of the Southern and Eastern rim of the Mediterranean basin and those of Northwest Europe was 3.3 to 1. The same ratio is during the 1990s expected to be around 17 to 1. Of the expected population increase in Europe and in the Mediterranean between 1990 and 2000, some 95 per cent will be represented by the Southern rim of the Mediterranean and only 5 per cent in the European Union (Commission 1990).

In 1990, 18.5 per cent of the population in the European Community was below 15 years of age, as compared to 37.5 per cent in the Maghreb area (OECD 1990), with consequences for the prospective number of newcomers in the labour market in the years to come. The fewer people absorbed in the local labour markets in the Maghreb area, the stronger would be the pressure on the major cities in the area,[50] and later the Northern rim of the Mediterranean.

Algeria, Tunisia, and Morocco already have a considerable part of their population living in Europe.

In recent years increasing numbers of people from these countries have moved to particularly Spain and Italy, also to France. Experts predict that these flows will increase even more in the years to come, although opinion differs on the likely magnitude. A weakness in many analyses is that too much one-sided emphasis is placed on demographic variables (OECD 1990).

Even though demographic imbalances and uneven level of development between nearby regions do have a notable effect on emigration pressure, there are still several unknown factors at work. In the final instance it is individuals who migrate, although their actions are often best understood in the context of the structural conditions surrounding them. Poverty

---

50. Within the Maghreb area, an urbanization rate of 40% is expected in the comming decade, with the creation of new jobs lagging significantly behind (Salt 1992).

and overpopulation are in themselves rarely sufficient explanations for emigration, a fact rarely mentioned when pictures of the "hungry hordes" are painted in the Western press.

The illegal migration which the West is now experiencing from the areas south of the Mediterranean is not a typical poverty-induced migration,[51] even though scarce openings in the labour market and gloomy prospects for the younger generations definitely represent central driving forces. The South–North "welfare gap" demarcated by the Mediterranean is obviously a part of this picture. Young people in this Southern area have better access to information on conditions in Europe than ever before, through films, TV programmes and not least through direct messages from people who have already migrated. Youth in these sending areas are enticed to expect more, at the same time as the possibilities of getting their expectations satisfied are slight.[52] The short distance across the sea, the openings in the unofficial labour market in Europe and the network linkages make the journey a lottery which can seem well worth trying for a number of people every year. The strength of these "push" factors are not expected to diminish in the years to come.

Refugees
As concerns politically induced immigration to Europe, in the form of asylum seekers, the origin areas are harder to predict. Refugee streams can, in principle, arrive from all corners of the world where people are exposed to war, civil war, violence, and violations of human rights. However, a distinction is made between those who can find protection in their own general area of the world, and those who flee long distances to find refuge. For refugees under UNHCR protection, the inter-

---

51. According to investigation undertaken by the Spanish union UGT, 25% of the illegal immigrants in the coastal city Almeria had university education (*Migration News Sheet* July 1991).
52. Recent research at the local level has revealed that young women *legally residing* in Europe have an exceedingly high value on the marriage market in the countries of origin (Amersfoort and Penninx 1994).

Table 9. Stock of North African residents in selected OECD countries (1988)

	Algeria	Morocco	Tunisia	Total	% of North African in relation to the total foreign population
Belgium	10,647	135,464	6,244	152,355	17.5
France *	820,900	516,400	202,600	1 539,900	41.0
Germany	5,100	52,100	21,600	78,800	−1.7
Italy	–	14,596	23,549	–	–
Netherlands	700	139,200	2,700	142,600	22.9
Spain	0	11,996	255	12,251	−3.4
Switzerland **	2,000	1,800	2,500	6,300	−0.6

* 1985. Includes children born in France to Algerian parents (approximately 290,000)
** Seasonal and Frontier workers are not included
Source: OECD (SOPEMI) Annual Report 1993

national community has established a reception and assistance apparatus, through which the refugees are contained in their own region. Mozambican refugees in Malawi and Zimbabwe, and Afghan refugees in Pakistan are examples of this policy. There are consequently insignificant numbers of asylum seekers in Western Europe from these areas. *Spontaneous* refugees, in many contexts, do not have the possibility of finding equivalent UNHCR protection locally. Various independent organizations, argue that few spontaneous refugees who arrive in Europe, USA, Canada and Australia *can* find UNHCR protection other places, and least of all in their own regions. Iranians, Iraqis, stateless Palestinians, and Lebanese are cited as typical examples in this respect (see, e.g. Christensen and Kjærum 1991; World Council of Churches 1991).

As long as safe arrangements are not established regionally, as long as the number of conflicts and repressive regimes are not reduced globally, and as long as one of the very few legal channels to Europe is the asylum path, pressure will persist on the European democracies to receive spontaneous refugees.

The escalation of the asylum-seeker flow is a major reason why the EU member-states have started making efforts to find common solutions as to control policies. Asylum questions now have top priority on the list of issues to be addressed and tentatively harmonized (see Chapter 4).

"Pull factors"

In the migration literature it is often held that activation of "push" factors requires that "pull" factors are present. To a certain extent this is obvious: There has to be some attraction in another area, unless the migrant is literally pressed out of his/her own locality. There is, however, reason to ask how *concretely* the potential migrant has to envisage the attraction, in other words, how much information is needed to uproot people if conditions in the sending area are felt as highly onerous. The ideal-type refugee will hardly have any choice; he or she must leave to avoid infringement. In this context the "pull" forces are nearly unimportant beyond the need for basic human rights protection. In the recent refugee debate in Europe it is argued that the "pull" forces now play a significant role for *spontaneous* refugees, who in practical terms are the only ones seen as problematic for the respective European authorities. In this argument there is also a judgement to the effect that non-political matters are contained in the "push" forces.

When it comes to *illegal* immigration from the South (as from the East), the "pull" forces play a more clear-cut role. The material attraction of Western Europe is striking, as is the contrast to the home areas of the migrants. The vision of a better life as well as the information flow telling that "nearly everybody" finds work on the other side, contributes to sustaining this attraction. Such migration is basically motivated by economic factors.[53]

---

53. Although even this migration has other dimensions which are not purely economic. Family security and long-term life chances are other preoccupations which can also be spelled out in non-economic terms.

It is difficult to foresee any short-term changes on the "pull" side in this context. In the longer run, what could diminish the illegal flows, would be a structural change in the labour market and a more efficient control policy (external and/or internal) which together would discourage employers from taking on unregistered labour. Combating illegal immigration is now a top item on the agenda in international fora dealing with migration. It remains to be seen which specific measures governments will come up with, apart from more police control at the borders and inside the countries.

After 1989 some analysts anticipated a reduction in the hiring of illegal labour from the South due to increased access to labour from Eastern Europe (reflected in, e.g. *Financial Times*, 12 March 1990). So far there has been little evidence to support this hypothesis (again stressing limitations in terms of data). It is not clear that immigrants from the East satisfy the same demand in the market as those from the South. Nor is it obvious that the influxes affect the same geographical areas in Europe.

The political level – prospects for South–North migration
As with the East–West migration, politics play an important part in the constitution and continuation of South–North migration patterns, although the results of official policies do not always go in the intended direction, as seen in Europe after the "immigration stop" of the early 1970s. Since migrants from the South have, by and large, had the freedom to emigrate, and since the colonial history of greater parts of Western Europe has brought about lasting migration "bridges", the Southern influx to Europe has been of another magnitude and significance.

As will be discussed in the next chapter, when it comes to the possibilities of controlling and handling immigration to Western Europe, much will depend on the political will and capability of the EU governments to come to terms with the most central dilemmas attached to the issue, and to coordinate/harmonize their efforts. The heavy concentration on *control* (first and foremost entry control, yet also internal control mechanisms) in the EU countries individually reflects a crisis reaction that does not tackle the more basic problems involved. In the longer run concerted efforts to influence both the structural "push" and the "pull" forces are absolutely necessary.

Regardless of what kind of policy the EU countries manage to formulate, the refugee flows and the irregular immigration from the South are likely to continue. As is the case with the East–West migration, very few experts dare to predict the magnitude of the flows, yet most believe that the pressure from the South also in the future will be of another scale than that from the East. The "sending" countries cover a much larger territory and the poverty problem is greater, relatively and in an absolute sense.

The Mahgreb area has so far played a special role in irregular immigration, and will probably continue to do so. This means that the Southern European countries will be most strongly affected, even after the introduction of the Internal Market. When it comes to asylum-seekers, the Union countries will in principle be more equal as potential receiving countries, considering the tendency to standardize asylum policies among the member-states. In practice, however, when *policies* are more equal, other factors will emerge as more decisive, like network, language, and climate.

Chapter 4

Towards Convergence of European Migration Policies

Immigration policy so far has basically been a *national* preoccupation, even though migration for quite some time has had strong inter-statal implications.[54] The increased globalization of the market place, internationalization of decision making and the regionalization of flows have reduced the autonomy of each state.

In Western Europe, the Internal Market, with the planned dismantling of internal border controls, gives every single member-state a clear interest in the immigration policies of its fellow member-states. Each state is vulnerable to the policies of the others.[55] One could think that this vulnerability would make immigration issues a prime candidate for transference to supra-national decision making. When this is not the case, it has to do with what Paul Kapteyn calls "the European dilemma": "fear of their weak national position leads these countries to join forces, yet it is the same fear which holds

---

54. As Miller and Mitchell have pointed out, immigration policy making in most Western European countries is assigned to ministries of the interior, labour and social affairs, a fact which suggests that Europeans regard immigration as a domestic policy issue (Miller and Mitchell 1993).

55. Immigration issues have also ranked high in negotiations between the European Union and some of the states seeking entry. Swiss negotiations with the Union have, e.g. involved extensive discussions about Swiss seasonal labour policy (Tomasi and Miller 1993).

them back" (Kapteyn 1992). I will in the following give some substance to this dilemma.

Historically, states have had to rely on control of national frontiers for their own security. Border control has been seen as a shield against terrorism, international crime, drug trafficking, illegal weapon trading – and immigration. The prospects of removing this national instrument have called forth claims for compensatory measures, both in terms of reinforced controls at the Community's external borders, and through strengthened *internal* (national) control mechanisms.

Immigration of third country nationals is not covered by the 1957 Treaty of Rome, which fosters free movement of persons *within* the EU area, but excepts non-EU citizens. In the 1987 revision of the Treaty of Rome, article 8a reads, "The internal market shall comprise an area without internal frontiers in which the free movement of goods, persons, services and capital is ensured in accordance with the provisions of this Treaty" (EEC Treaty 1987).

At present, the lack of consensus on the interpretation of this article represents a major barrier to a common immigration policy in the Community. Some member countries, particularly the UK and Denmark, firmly interpret "free movement of persons" to mean EU citizens only. The European Commission, on the other hand, clearly states the general application of the article: "The phrase 'free movement of ... all persons' in Article 8a refers to all persons, whether or not they are economically active and irrespective of their nationality. The internal market could not operate under conditions equivalent to those in a national market if the movement of individuals within this market were hindered by controls at internal frontiers" (Commission 1992a).

Immigration of third-country nationals in a way disturbs the philosophical basis of the Community. Free movement of labour is one of the constituting elements of the EEC Treaty, yet third-country nationals are *de facto* not yet included in this basis. The legal status of third-country nationals living in an EU member-state (resident aliens) is not contained in the Single European Act, even though this group now constitutes the majority of the immigrant population in Western Europe. Around 13 million immigrants are now living in the EU countries. 8 million of these (2.5 per cent of total EU population) are third-country nationals – predominantly from North Africa, Turkey, former Yugoslavia and the Indian sub-continent (Martin et al. 1991).

A senior official in the European Commission, G. Callovi, asks, "Will not firms' competitiveness in a free economic and trade area be threatened if third-country labour does not enjoy, in all member states, equality of treatment with national labour?" (Callovi 1992:368). Others argue that it would be "against economic rationality to have a single European market with 12 different policies towards non-EU residents, limiting their labour mobility to within the territory of one single member state and requiring them to apply for entry visas and work permits for other member-states. This would result in the inefficient use of manpower and would give rise to problems such as the case of firms having to provide services or operating in two or more member-states. This would, moreover, aggravate the discrimination between Community and non-Community nationals, thus reinforcing the already tarnished image of a Community with second or even third class citizens which is contrary to the democratic values which member-states purport to uphold" (Cruz 1991b:14).

The core of the matter concerning Article 8a (now changed to 7a in the Maastricht Treaty) is how to control the movements of non-EU residents without simultaneously controlling those of EU nationals. Despite the heated discussions over Article 8a, and the reluctance to transfer competence to the supra-national level in the area of immigration, the enhanced freedom of movement with the Single Market has stimulated a tendency towards greater cooperation and coordination between EU member countries in this field.

The historical account

The first time the word "Community" appeared alongside "migration policy" was in a Communication from the Commission to the Council entitled "Guidelines for a Community Policy on Migration", on 1 March 1985 (Callovi 1992).

Since then, migration policy has rather quickly developed into a central theme for the Community. Pressed by events (the collapse of the Eastern Bloc and the crisis in former Yugoslavia) and long-term processes (population growth and the widening economic gap North–South) the EU member-states have had to investigate new instruments for tackling immigration. The establishment of the Internal Market has stepped up the pace of this development.

The 1987 Single European Act implied, as we have noted, the dismantling of all intra-EU border control as a facilitator for the free movement of people (Article 8a). The question of migration is, in the context of this act, related to the removal of border controls, and the problems attached to this. A White Paper issued together with the Act introduced a series of measures on immigration aimed at the realization of the Internal Market in 1993. Among these measure were proposals for Community *Directives* on the coordination of visa policics, the status of non-EU residents, and the rules for granting asylum and refugee status. The White Paper from the European Commission was adopted by the Council in Milan in June 1985. However, as specific proposals for these Directives were formulated, opposition to transferring competence to the Community in these fields became clearer, particularly on issues concerning rules of entry and asylum (Cruz 1991a). The Single Act was accompanied by the "Political Declaration by the Governments of the Member-States on the free movement of people, in which authority over ... the entry, movement and residence of nationals of third countries" was preserved for the Member-States. The twelve had already individually started the process of compensating for the abolition of border control. By 1988 the Commission had to give in to the pressure from the member-states, and settle on a more "pragmatic" line to keep the timetable for 1992 (Commission 1988).

The dilemma for the EU member-states is that elaborated cooperation is absolutely necessary due to the international character of the phenomenon and the dependence on mutual confidence in the whole EU process, yet at the same time migration touches upon a whole range of sensitive *national* issues where authority is not easily entrusted to other levels of decision making.

As a consequence of the reluctance to harmonize immigration-related policies among member-states, various inter-governmental bodies and agreements have been established.

Schengen
The most significant inter-governmental arrangement in this respect is the Schengen Agreement, first signed in June 1985 between the Benelux countries, Germany, and France, and later joined by Italy in 1990, by Spain and Portugal in 1991, and Greece in 1992. This means that up to January 1 1995 only Denmark, the United Kingdom, and Eire did not participate in the group among the EU member countries. After 1 January 1995 three new member countries, Austria, Sweden, and Finland, joined the Union. As a result of the stronger Nordic participation in the Union, Denmark has joined forces with Finland and Sweden in negotiating an agreement with the Schengen countries. It is not yet clear (as of October 1995) what will be the outcome of these negotiations, as Norway's non-member status (both in the Union and in Schengen) poses a problem, due to the long-existing Nordic Passport Union. As a consequence of this problem, Norway is currently negotiating an attachment status to the Schengen Agreement.[56] The

---

56. This matter is, however, highly controversial in the Norwegian population, which only one year ago (November 1994), voted down membership in the European Union in a referendum. A Schengen affiliation could easily be seen as a «sneaking in the backdoor» strategy by the Government.

aim of the agreement was to abolish controls at the common borders of the participating countries by 1 January 1990. This idea was not originally motivated by the desire to restrict immigration, but was pushed forward by a protest movement of lorry drivers (1984) tired of the long queues at internal European borders. Along the way, more and more restrictive policies towards immigrants became a part of the negotiations leading up to the signing of the Schengen Agreement (Cruz 1993).

In 1988 and 1989 the original signatory countries discussed an extended agreement which would also deal with policy towards asylum seekers. This "Schengen Supplementary Agreement" was then endorsed in June 1990, as a convention on the application of the Schengen Agreement. It was designed to accelerate the creation of a region without internal borders, and to provide effective means to compensate for their disappearance. The main components of the agreement are,

- common rules for control at external borders of the Schengen area;
- adjustment of conditions for border crossing and visa policy;
- sanctions against air companies which carry people without proper documents;
- criteria for which country should handle asylum applications;
- exchange of information on asylum seekers.

The agreement is meant to gradually abolish internal border controls among the signatory states, at the same time reinforcing controls at the external borders of the area. When the internal border control is dismantled, internal civil control with main roads, railway stations, and harbours will be stepped up. Any non-Schengen foreigners who do not qualify for entry should be turned back at the border. The agreement specifies, however, that the rules are not to inhibit the application of the special conditions attached to the right to apply for asylum (Article 5, Chapter 7). The basic rule is that the country which has issued a visa or has accepted entry, is responsible for handling the application. The same applies to applications for family reunification.

The agreement also includes cooperation in the field of police operations, security, and information (Schengen Information System, SIS). The data system provides the authorities with information, not only about persons who are convicted or suspected of serious offences against public law, but also about individuals who have been refused entry, expelled, deported, etc. Thus, the data system SIS and the agreement imply that authorities may exchange information about the individual asylum seeker, in terms of identity, travel route, previous applications etc. Other information – like the reasons for applying, and the basis for the decision taken by the authorities – may be transferred in cases where the authorities find it advisable, yet only with the asylum seeker's consent. The asylum seeker has the right to have a print-out of the information, and the right to have it annulled in case of mistakes or inaccuracies. A central objection in this respect concerns the likelihood of asylum seekers being informed about these rights in specific situations. Generally speaking, there has been criticism that protection of information about individuals is insufficient. The criticism from the Committee on Civil Liberties and Internal Affairs in the European Parliament has, for example, been quite harsh: "One cannot escape the impression that police services are in a sense exploiting the internationalization of the maintenance of law and order to increase their powers or acquire new ones which they would probably not be granted by their own national parliaments.... More than anybody else, representatives of ministries of justice and police forces ... have seized control of the Schengen process" (European Parliament 1992:20).

Another criticism raised has been that the Schengen agreement lacks provisions for supra-national judicial control which could impose sanctions in case of abuses or malpractice on the part of the national authorities.

The Schengen Agreement was intended as a "pilot project" for the development of an EU response to immigration, and it was supposed to be realized far in advance of the Internal Market. The European Commission had anticipated that the agreement could draw up technical solutions to speed up the removal of border controls throughout the Community (Callovi 1992). The Commission participated from the beginning as an observer in the ministerial meetings of Schengen. Ironically, the initiative was blocked by internal problems and disagreement, so that it took more than two years after the opening of the Internal Market, before the Schengen Agreement was ready for implementation, on 26 March 1995. Even after this date, however, France quickly signalled that the «compensatory measures» were not good enough for France to abolish border controls. Late in the spring 1995 France imposed a halt in the process, and announced delays in abandoning border checks. The recent bomb explosions in Paris have made the government even more alerted to the border-control question.

A basic problem has all along been the question of drug traffic. In France the major stumbling block has been what is perceived as liberal drug laws in the Netherlands, Spain, and possibly also Italy. French politicians have been clear in their message: there will be no suppression of internal frontiers unless the Schengen partners apply the same restrictive external border control as France (Cruz 1993). Besides, beyond Schengen, within the EU there are different interpretations of Article 8a of the EEC Treaty, as we have seen. The non-Schengen countries, Denmark, the United Kingdom, and Ireland do not share the view that internal border control should have been eradicated by the realization of the Internal Market.

Intergovernmental bodies
Alongside increased immigration to Western Europe during the 1980s, there has been a proliferation of intergovernmental bodies dealing with the issue from various angles. Towards the end of 1988 the member-states consequently felt the need to coordinate the activities, and, at a European Council meet-

ing at Rhodes in December 1988, it was decided to establish the Group of Coordinators on the Free Movement of Persons (The "Rhodes Group"), consisting of senior officials of the member-states as well as representatives of the European Commission, responsible for supervising of the process of implementing free movement of persons. The Rhodes Group was meant to coordinate the work of the following bodies:

the Ad Hoc Immigration Group;
the Trevi Groups;
the Mutual Assistance Group (MAG);
the European Committee to Combat Drugs (CELAD);
the European Political Cooperation Group (EPC);
the Horizontal Group.[57]

The initial task of the Group of Coordinators was to elaborate a timetable of measures and a close monitoring of the intergovernmental bodies to secure the respect for deadlines (Cruz 1991a). The following year (1989), the group drew up a list of measures seen as preconditions for the dismantling of border controls, the so-called "Palma Document". These measures included proposals for two conventions: one on asylum questions and one on the crossing of external borders. Both conventions were to be handled by the Ad Hoc group.

Two conventions
The Ad Hoc Immigration Group, set up in 1986 by the Council, consisted of ministers responsible for immigration (home affairs and justice). The group was assisted by a working party of senior civil servants. The Ad Hoc Group prepared its proceedings in five sub-groups: asylum; external borders; false papers; entry expulsion; and exchange of information.

So far the text of the two conventions has been formulated by the group. The first, the Dublin Convention (1990), relates

---

57. For a more elaborate overview of the activities of these bodies, see Cruz (1993).

to the right of asylum. This convention defines the rules for ensuring that every application for asylum is examined. It designates the criteria to be used in determining which member-state shall be responsible for undertaking this examination. It seeks to avoid multiple applications submitted by a single asylum seeker in more than one state, and what is called "refugees in orbit" – a situation where no state accepts responsibility for an asylum seeker. The rules for the substantial examining of the asylum requests continue to be covered by the national law of each member-state of the Community. This is the same arrangement as in the Schengen Agreement. The intention of the Dublin Convention is exclusively to regulate relations between the member-states by designating their mutual obligations. Yet by drawing up rules which imply that every signatory state approves of transferring to another state applications submitted to their own state, the convention presupposes mutual confidence in the realm of asylum policies (Ad Hoc Group 1991). Concerning *procedure*, all the involved states (Schengen and Dublin) have agreed to maintain their respective *national* methods for the handling of applications (Joly 1993). The Dublin convention is to enter into force three months after ratification by *all* member-states. As of January 1995, only six of the EU states had finalized this stage; Greece, the United Kingdom, Denmark, Italy, Luxembourg, and Portugal.

The exchange of information is central in both the Dublin Convention and the Schengen Agreement. Relevant and important information includes general information on national procedures; various statistical data on monthly arrivals (nationality, changing patterns, individual data in terms of family members, etc.); itineraries; former decisions taken, etc. (Joly 1993). A Clearing House (CIREA) has been established to take care of information exchange. This "informal forum", consisting of representatives from the EU member-countries, was initiated by the Ad Hoc Group and endorsed by the Maastricht summit.

The second convention drawn up by the Ad Hoc Group, the Border Convention, deals with conditions for crossing of frontiers external to the *Union*, and for issuing visas. It includes provisions for recognition of national visas among the member-states, and the elimination of visa requirements for third-country nationals legally resident in one member-state for a period of less than three months. This makes it easier for legal immigrants to stay in other member-states for more limited periods. Consequently, the convention encourages a common visa policy within the EU area (Commission 1991). On the other hand, there may be an increased possibility of legal immigrants taking up residence in another member-state as employees or self-employed persons. This process, may, according to the Ad Hoc Group, lead to certain tension and pressure on *national* immigration policies (Ad Hoc Group 1991). The Border Convention also provides for cooperation on expulsion policy. This field again illustrates the tension between the national and international level of decision making: According to the Border Convention, member-states are generally responsible for escorting illegal aliens to the EU borders. If, however, one of the member-states should subsequently re-admit the same foreigner with reference to *national* immigration policy, the expulsion loses its validity, and "co-operation between member-states would be impaired" (ibid.:12).

A computerized list of *persona non grata* is proposed in connection with the Border Convention.

The Ad Hoc Group itself sees the "ultimate effect" of the two conventions as "much greater than was perhaps originally expected", and it views harmonization of at least basic asylum policy merely as a "logical step" forward (Ad Hoc Group 1991:12). Generally speaking, the effects of the Border Convention are seen as "considerably improved" if *immigration policies* of the member-states could be harmonized (ibid.:13)

The Border Convention has, however, not yet been agreed upon due to the still unsettled conflict between the United Kingdom and Spain over the border between Spain and Gibraltar.[58]

---

58. The Spanish government considers the border to be external whereas the UK government considers it *internal*.

The two conventions as well as the Schengen Agreement have been strongly criticized by various humanitarian organizations as well as the European Parliament. The latter has been opposed to the fact that the conventions have been elaborated and concluded outside the Community mechanism, and hence outside the control or influence of the Parliament itself. According to the Parliament (and various NGOs[59]), the conventions do not offer sufficient protection of human rights. The European Commission adds to this criticism: "We feel it prudent to emphasize in this regard, that imposing severe restrictions on the free movement of third-country migrants may be discriminatory in the sense of too great a discrepancy between the rights of the nationals and of foreigners, especially those who have been resident for some time" (Commission 1990:37).

The Trevi Group

The Trevi Group, formed in Rome in 1976, consisted of Ministers of Justice and Home Affairs as well as senior civil servants responsible for law enforcement. It was founded as an intergovernmental body on police cooperation, initially aimed at fighting terrorism. The group has expanded its engagement to include problems related to illegal immigration. The Trevi Group has been divided into five sections. One of these, Trevi 92, was created in 1989 to handle consequences of the suppression of internal borders within the EU in terms of "lack of security". This group, dissolved by decision of the ministers in London, on 30 November 1992, made a programme of action for cooperation in police matters and in the fight against terrorism and other forms of organized crime (Cruz 1993). This programme, adopted by Trevi ministers in Dublin in 1990, also managed rules of police control at external borders, clandestine immigration, identification of undesirable aliens, as

---

59. Churches Committee for Migrants in Europe (CCME), the European Ecumenical Commission for Church and Society (EECCS), Immigration Law Practitioners' Association (ILPA), and others.

well as the establishment of the *European Information System* (EIS). This system is named "SIS of the Twelve", as it is meant to be almost identical to the information system of Schengen (Cruz 1993). The work of the Trevi Group has been equally criticized for its closed and secrecy-loaded character.

Generally speaking, the question of openness has increasingly come to the fore in the various fora related to immigration. The Ad Hoc Group recognized this fact in its report to the Maastricht summit, and admitted "insufficient transparency" in its work (Ad Hoc Group 1991:17). Even though secret decision making may be "efficient" in the sense that common ground can be reached more quickly among governmental representatives than by following the tedious parliamentary road, implementation requires a democratic foundation. In the context of the Ad Hoc Group, this has meant that the Commission and the UNHCR have been more regularly involved in discussions and preparations of policy proposals on asylum. This has taken the form of informal consultations and official meetings, like the "Troika" meetings with representatives of the EU Presidency, the Secretariat Council, the Commission, and UNHCR. Both the Schengen group and the Ad Hoc Group have asked for comments from the Commission, UNHCR, and even some NGOs like, e.g. ECRE (European Consultation on Refugees and Exiles) (Joly 1993).

The Maastricht Treaty

The European Council meeting in Luxembourg in June 1991 represented a new step in the process towards harmonization. The Council called for rapid agreement on the Convention on Crossing of External Borders, and agreed on the objectives underlying a proposal from the German government to the effect that a "formal and actual harmonization" could take place concerning policies on asylum, immigration and aliens. It was believed that current intergovernmental activities could be brought into the governance of the Union in the context of the European Council of Maastricht, to be held later the same year. In preparation for this event, the Commission drew up two communications: one on the right of asylum (11 October 1991) and one on immigration (23 October 1991) (Callovi 1992). Up to this point the efforts of the member-states and the Commission had been restricted to preparing the new forms of cooperation necessary to handle the situation after implementation of the frontier-free area on 1 January 1993. The two conventions were fruits of this approach. The invitation of the Luxembourg European Council to the ministers to transcend this limited objective reflected a (in the words of the Commission) recognition that "the geo-political and socio-economic background against which immigration and asylum issues had to be viewed was changing rapidly and called for a different level of co-operation than before, moving beyond procedure into substance" (Commission 1994:2).

The Maastricht Treaty of 1991 represents the most important building block in the European structure since the Treaty of Rome. Formally it reflects the political will of the Twelve to develop a common policy on immigration, as can be seen from Treaty provisions like Article 3d, 100c, Title VI, and the Declaration on Asylum. Article 3 of the Union Treaty incorporates measures related to entry and movement of persons in the internal market into the Community sphere. Under Article 100c, the Community will have the power to determine those countries whose nationals require a visa to cross the external borders of the Community. This is a question of clear legal competence transferred to the Community. The procedure for adoption will be by unanimous vote, until 1995, and with prior consultation of the European Parliament. Paragraph 7 of Article 100c nevertheless states that intergovernmental conventions are to remain in operation until their substance has been replaced by Community instruments.

Title VI (Provisions on Cooperation in the Fields of Justice and Home Affairs), states in article K1, "For the purpose of achieving the objectives of the Union, in particular the free movement of persons, and without prejudice to the powers of the European Community, Member-states shall regard the following areas as matters of common interest:

(1) asylum policy; (2) rules governing the crossing by persons of the external borders of the Member-States and the exercise of controls thereon; (3) immigration policy and policy regarding nationals of third countries: (a) conditions of entry and movement by nationals of third countries on the territory of Member-States; (b) conditions of residence by nationals of third countries on the territory of Member-States, including family reunion and access to employment; (c) combating unauthorized immigration, residence and work by nationals of third countries on the territory of Member-States; (4) combating drug addiction in so far as this is not covered by (7) to (9); (5) combating fraud on an international scale in so far as this is not covered by (7) to (9); (6) judicial cooperation in civil matters; (7) judicial cooperation in criminal matters; (8) customs cooperation; (9) police cooperation for the purpose of preventing and combating terrorism, unlawful drug trafficking and other serious forms of international crime, including if necessary certain aspects of customs cooperation, in connection with the organization of a Union-wide system for exchanging information within a European Police Office (Europol)." (Treaty on European Union 1991:131ff)

These points, which can be subject to common action, possibly by qualified majority, represent an extension of the areas covered by the Schengen Agreement. Article K3, paragraph 2b states that the Council may "adopt joint action in so far as the objectives of the union can be attained better by joint action than by the Member-States acting individually ... it may decide that measures implementing joint action are to be adopted by a qualified majority" (ibid.:133). Thus, in perhaps the majority of the cases, the issue will still be dealt with at the intergovernmental level. The procedure has nevertheless been amended with the power of initiative assigned to the Commission (on the first six topics) (Article K3); the information and consultation role assigned to the European Parliament (Article K6); the power of control granted to the Court of Justice (Article K3); and finally through Article K9, the entitlement of the Council (based on unanimous decision) to transfer certain matters (asylum, border crossing and immigration) to the area of Community competence.

The question of unanimity is important here. Given the current atmosphere created by real and anticipated immigration pressure on the EU external borders, it is not likely that *all* the governments would agree to relinquish control over their respective borders, without simultaneously *effectively* reinforcing the EU external borders.

For the above first six points, the Treaty foresees the Commission making proposals in order to coordinate the actions of member-states. The Council may respond to such proposals either by creating conventions/adopting joint action, or by deciding to apply Article 100c of the Treaty, i.e. transferring matters to this article (Callovi 1992). Despite the intergovernmental emphasis, a notable change has occurred: for the first time, "administrative expenditure" of the intergovernmental institutions "shall be charged to the budget of the European Communities" (Article K8, para. 2).[60]

In the Treaty on European Union, home and justice affairs belong under the so-called "third pillar", granting both member-states and the Commission the power of initiative; yet such activities will remain intergovernmental, apart from a common visa policy towards third-country nationals (Article 100c). Migration policy is related to all three "pillars" of the Union Treaty. In the first pillar, "Community matters", a new article is incorporated (as compared to the Treaty of Rome), to the effect that the Council of the European Community "shall determine the third countries whose nationals must be in possession of a visa crossing the external borders of the Member-

---

60. This point is made by Antonio Cruz (1993).

States", and, by 1 January 1996, "shall adopt the measures related to uniform format for visas". The second pillar, "foreign and security policy", is not directly related to immigration issues, but does have indirect and potential importance, as migration issues are increasingly discussed in terms of foreign policy and security. The third pillar, "justice and home affairs" covers a whole range of questions of "common interest" to member-states.

As of 1 November 1993, the date for the formal establishment of the European Union, the various inter-governmental bodies in charge of migration and asylum issues, were officially replaced by new structures. Their activities are now divided among three new bodies: Steering Committee I (migration and asylum issues – replacing the Ad Hoc Group); Steering Committee II (police matters previously dealt with by the Trevi Groups); and Steering Committee III (judicial cooperation) (*Migration News Sheet* November 1993). These three committees are to prepare statements and proposals. A new point is that they will forward these documents to the new Coordinating Committee (K 4 group), which has replaced the old Rhodes Group.

Post-Maastricht

The Community's institutions are, thus, not fully excluded from the inter-governmental process. The Maastricht Treaty lays down the rules of conduct for inter-governmental negotiations: certain decisions must be unanimous; the Commission is granted the right of initiative in certain areas; the European Parliament is to be informed of discussions and may make recommendations; agreements concluded through the inter-governmental processes *may* be brought under the jurisdiction of the Court of Justice, but need not be; and finally, new areas may be incorporated into the realm of EU decision making, provided there is unanimous agreement among the member-states (Dummett and Niessen 1993).

A more positive interpretation of the principles laid down by the Union Treaty is that the Union offers new opportunities for *developing policies* in relation to immigration and asylum, as a new single framework is provided for aspects of foreign and security policy (Title V), and of justice and home affairs (Title VI). In practice this may mean that a more comprehensive approach, including social policy, trade, security, development policy, management of integration, etc. can be catered for within a single institutional framework (Commission 1994). Thus, there is a new *potential* in the Treaty. The Commission itself says in the 1994 Communication: "The move from *ad hoc* intergovernmental cooperation, theoretically reversible at any moment, to a Treaty commitment to cooperate on a permanent basis nevertheless constitutes a considerable political signal both to public opinion in Member-states and to the outside world" (Commission 1994:6). The critical question is how to interpret the term "commitment", and how this will be spelled out in practical terms in contentions between the member-states. The Commission itself sees the new structure as representing "possible instruments" (ibid.:6) and states that the development of common rules and practices is still at a preliminary stage (ibid.:9).

In sum then, despite the declaration of intention and the good will expressed in terms of (long-term) harmonization of immigration policies in the Maastricht Treaty, the specific measures were vague and non-binding on central issues. Consequently, the basic signal is that member governments still want to retain real control over immigration questions.[61] The Maastricht Treaty consolidated the inter-governmental rather than the federal approach to immigration issues. It did not

---

61. According to a Eurobarometer survey (June 1993), this is against the will of the majority of EU citizens: 60% of respondents favoured having immigration policy treated at the EU level (35% against). Concerning asylum policies, 61% preferred EU authority (33% against). The survey revealed that a sizable majority wanted the European Parliament to have priority in deciding on matters of immigration policy (73% in favour, 18% against) and of asylum (70% in favour, 21% against) (referred from *Migration News Sheet* August 1993).

succeed in profoundly strengthening the role of the Commission and the European Parliament.[62]

The European Community as such is founded on the principle of binding Community legislation, interpreted by the European Court of Justice and protected by the Commission. Any offended citizen may appeal against a faulty application or lack of application of Community law. If necessary the Court of Justice will provide binding interpretation. In the case of immigration policy now, with the Maastricht Treaty, Title IV grants the Commission a co-initiative power with the member-states in the majority of issues dealt with under the "third pillar" (Article K3). This right, however, applies only to joint opinions, joint action and conventions: it does not provide the Commission with the right to present proposals for directives and regulations. Resolutions and recommendations adopted by the ministers responsible for immigration are not legally binding on the member-states; yet they are, according to EU Commissioner Flynn,[63] "not without importance or effect as they have both a political and moral weight which member-states will always be slow to ignore" (*Migration News Sheet* August 1993:2). In his view, Title VI does represent an advance for both the Commission and Parliament "whatever its imperfections" (ibid.:1).

The European Commission
This leads to the role of the European Commission and the interplay between the various protagonists in the process. There has been a subtle movement within the European Community as to the balance between inter-governmental and su-

---

62. The European Parliament has nevertheless become more active in the sphere of migration. Several studies have been commissioned in recent years, and in November 1992 the Parliament adopted two significant resolutions in response to the Commission's 1991 Communications on Immigration and Asylum (A3-0280/92 and A3-0337/92). These resolutions taken together present a separate action programme for the Parliament on migration and asylum policies. The general line is a generous approach to immigrants and asylum seekers together with a strict policy against irregular immigration.
63. At a European Parliament meeting on 15 July 1993.

pra-national power. According to G. Callovi, the Commission has been fully aware of the delicate nature of this balance, and it has considered "that attention should be focused on practical effectiveness rather than on matters of legal doctrine" (Callovi 1992:360). On the other hand, the Commission would not wish to "rule out the possibility of coming forward with additional proposals, particularly if it becomes clear that inter-governmental cooperation is not the most efficient or cost-effective method, or if a consensus were to emerge among member-states that further harmonization and coordination is desirable" (ibid.). It seems that the Commission is in abeyance, as it were, letting events create their own impetus.

Before the Maastricht Council meeting in December 1991, the Commission presented its own broad framework for a Community policy on immigration (Commission 1991). The main elements of this "global" policy, which seeks to "combine realism with solidarity" (ibid.:2), are:

1) Action on migration pressure: migration should be made an integral part of the Community's external policy in terms of cooperation with countries of emigration, especially developing countries, "to strike the right balance between immediate measures and demographic trends" (ibid.:2)

2) Controlling migration flows: "Without seeking to prejudge the question of the member-states' capacity for absorbing migrants (which, in some cases, would seem to have reached its limits), and on the basis of an agreed stance on migration flows, the point must be to control existing immigration channels, bearing in mind the fact that all member-states have now adopted restrictive provisions: measures to combat illegal immigration, a joint approach to the right of asylum, approximation of criteria for reuniting families, formulation of a joint code on temporary contracts" (ibid.:2–3).

3) Strengthening integration policies for the benefit of legal immigrants: "Action at Community level can boost the

chances of success of national integration policies, in themselves an essential element in terms of guaranteeing democracy and solidarity" (ibid.:3).

This outline for a comprehensive policy also caters to longterm aspects of the migration complex: the root causes and the question of integration. It must be seen as an answer to the rather heavy concentration on external control policies undertaken by the respective member-states and inter-governmental bodies. This three-point approach was reiterated in the latest Communication from the Commission to the Council and the European Parliament (Commission 1994). This Communication is to be read as a new push toward a more complex European immigration policy.[64] It goes beyond the existing work programme of the Union (the European Council Plan of Action of December 1993) to put forward "new ideas and a new emphasis on how policy objectives can be pursued in operational terms" (Commission 1994:1b). The document sums up achievements in the area since the introduction of the work plan triggered off by the Maastricht meeting. "Harmonization" (in the sense of "common rules and practices") is said still to linger at a preliminary stage. "Approximation" has accordingly been introduced as a more appropriate term for the time being, as the resolutions adopted by immigration ministers are not of a legally binding nature and "their interpretation is left to each member state" (Commission 1994:9). Additionally, it is stated that no attempt has been made to create a mechanism to monitor implementation of these reso-

---

64. As apposed to the former round of communications from the Commission to the Council in this area, immigration and asylum issues are this time presented together in one document. The separation of the two in 1991 was "intended to underline the humanitarian basis of asylum rights as distinct from questions raised by immigration issues in general" (Commission 1994:1). In the introduction to the 1994 Communication, the Commission states that this distinction still holds valid as in 1991. It is, nevertheless, seen as increasingly difficult to examine immigration and asylum separately. This decision, although controversial within the Commission, should be seen as a political signal to the effect that the two fields are increasingly inter-related, and must be tackled accordingly.

lutions. According to the Commission, achieving and implementing a common policy on asylum and immigration will not be possible without "greater reliance on legally binding instruments, procedures to ensure uniform interpretation of those common rules and the development of common policies in relation to areas of both substantive and procedural law that have not yet been addressed (some of which will probably prove to be the most sensitive)" (ibid.:10).

There is no doubt that a comprehensive, long-term strategy of the kind the Commission is proposing is necessary for dealing with the substantive issues. Yet, as the Commission itself states, "no international forum has yet proved capable of making such a policy operational" (ibid.:11). The Commission believes that the Union now has the institutional means to do so.

The Commission, of course, has an interest in gaining control over more political territory. It is easier to act upon a question when one controls more of the premises; besides, successive inclusion of fields into the Community realm is a part of the general logic of the Community process. On the other hand, the Commission is correct in saying that there is *no other* international forum suited for the complex task of managing migration in a humanitarian way which is at the same time politically feasible. Whether the European Community will be able to serve this purpose, depends on the complicated and time-consuming power struggle at many levels, within and between member-states. We might witness a process where governments realize that the advantages of inter-governmental cooperation (with a relatively short drafting process) are countervailed by the disadvantages, such as the protracted ratification procedures involved (Dummet and Niessen 1993).

Strength through pragmatism?
As noted, the Commission proposals to the Maastricht Summit were far from accepted. This has meant a continuation of what Commissioner Bangemann has labelled a "pragmatic rather than doctrinary" approach (European Parliament 1991:6).

What is this pragmatism? Does it reflect what the so-called Malangre Report characterizes as the "continuous fewer ambitions of the Commission" (European Parliament 1991:14)? This is largely a question of power and conflicting interests during a vulnerable formation process. The European Commission, lacking extensive formal competence in immigration matters, becomes a restricted and somewhat subtle actor. To avoid becoming merely a well-intended resolution maker the Commission has to avoid proposals that are obviously doomed to lose in confrontation with the member-states.[65] At the first meeting of the Justice and Internal Affairs Council on 29–30 November 1993, a Report of the Commission to the Council dealt with the possibility of applying Article K9 of the Treaty on European Union to asylum policy (SEC(93) 1687 final), i.e. bringing *asylum* policies under Community competence (application of Article 100c). The report cited a whole range of advantages – transparency, a full involvement of the European Parliament, possibly more rapid decision making, and a wider range of policy instruments (regulations, directives, decisions).[66] All the same, the Commission concluded that "the time is not yet right ... so soon after the entry into force of the Treaty on the European Union", and adds that the issue should be re-examined "in the light of experience" later on.

Is then the Commission weak in its handling of migration issues? The question of the political and structural strength of the Commission is not easily determined. According to Yasemin Soysal, the Commission has a "weak authoritative structure ... but an increasing level of activity, organization and standardization around this weak structure. The trend (in immigration policy area) has not been to replace national legislation by a set of authoritative EU rules, but to specify certain abstract principles, which in turn create a common discourse

---

65. "This would render the Commission without credibility in the longer run, and very little would have been achieved" (statement by a senior official in the Commission, 1992).
66. The reference here is to the Dublin Convention, which has been ratified by only six member states five years after it was signed.

of policy and practice" (Soysal 1992). Through this approach, the principal sovereignty of the respective nation-states is not confronted. For the time being, given the structural limitations, the Commission cannot push issues any further than to the maximum of what the member-states can jointly agree upon. Yet the function as an "agenda setter" (ibid.) gives potential strength. The current pragmatism of the European Commission is an acknowledgement of the structural limitations. According to G. Callovi, a discussion of the doctrinary issues would have been "political suicide". "If the Commission were to submit to the Council draft directives or regulations, then the fight on competence would be initiated. Thus, tactically, it appeared more appropriate to recall the objectives and commitments subscribed by member-states in signing the Single European Act, and to let the intergovernmental co-operation find its own solutions" (Callovi 1990:17).

On the other hand, the mere existence of the Community influences the policy of its individual member-states. The Community does have a significant *indirect* impact through the fact that governments have to consider the other states' policy due to the international character of current migration flows. It is a question of mutual expectations which might become self-fulfilling prophecies: The existence of the European Union implies that central actors *assume* (even without supranational competence) that the EU countries as a group will end up with a clearly restrictive line on immigration. Everybody is afraid of the "magnet effect", which in practice means that the policy of the most restrictive state will set the tone.

Besides, individual governments may use the EU process as a shield against their own national opinion; arguing that a certain policy is necessary to conform with the other member countries, and with the expected future policy of the Community.[67]

The EU states are thus "mutual hostages": the EU authority

---

67. The recent amendment of the German Constitution is an example of this.

does not fully represent a *third party*, yet it constitutes a "strong implicit expectation" shared by the member countries (Kapteyn 1991:379).[68]

Differences between the member-states in terms of immigration policy have clearly *diminished* along with a common concern to restrict the overall line. Yet, the process towards a (tentatively) "enclosed" Community has not been conducted from Brussels. If one may speak of a wanted "Fortress Europe", this development is not a result of a supranational policy process imposed from above. The drift towards stricter control throughout Europe has come about through a combination of successive tougher measures presented by individual member-states as well as various inter-governmental initiatives aimed at a convergence of policy and practice.

There remains a striking need for a common long-term European policy. It is out of the reach of any single EU country to handle the situation alone, and to turn the downward spiral leading to successively tougher policies. The way immigration is handled today may thwart European integration as such. As Gary Freeman puts it: "the *failure* of the states to deal with the crisis may [ironically] reinforce *national* prerogatives and capacities with respect to immigration" (Freeman 1992: 1144). On the other hand, this failure can also be seen as a result of tensions and contradictions at the *national* level. In the following the dynamics on the national scene will be analysed through three central parameters within the immigration field: the need for control; forces in the labour market; and efforts to integrate foreigners into society.

---

68. Paul Kapteyn was applying this analytical point in connection with the Schengen Agreement, but it is equally relevant at the EU level.

Chapter 5

The External–Internal Boundary Building Complex

This book has, so far, firstly discussed the more principle foundation and the historical generation of immigration control in Europe; secondly assessed various possible scenarios as to the future immigration to Western Europe; and thirdly analysed the new dilemmas confronting the member-states of the European Union as a result of the Internal Market and the drive towards a stronger integration of the immigration policies of the Union.

Let us now move on from the sketchy, three-part model (push, pull, and politics) used in Chapter 3 to some of the structural and institutional forces that influence actors in the migration complex, East–West and South–North.

Immigration control exercised by sovereign states in essence has a dual aim of regulating both the entry of foreign citizens to its territory, and their access to residence and the labour market. The vigour with which this control is exercised has varied according to the historical context.

External vs. internal control

So far, the formal control mechanism – the historical development of the context for immigration control undertaken by nation-states – has been focused. Yet nation-states play an important but not exclusive role concerning today's immigration policies. On the one hand, non-official actors within society on different levels and across borders serve to limit the effectiveness of control policies; control policies are often altered or adjusted by counteractions of other actors in the process. On the other hand, more subtle internal control mechanism may *supplement* and even reinforce the public course. As to the immigrants, they are subject to gatekeeping mechanisms at many levels, beginning with physical barriers in terms of borders. If these barriers are surpassed, new formal and informal hindrances appear; the formal ones relate to accesses to basic needs, rights, and work whereas the informal ones apply to the vague *clôture sociale* (Leca 1992) – social mechanisms that determine the limits to participation or exclusion in the realm of civil society.

It has been convincingly argued that there is an *interplay* between external and internal control mechanisms. Michael Walzer (1983) has claimed that societies can be open only if borders are at least potentially closed, whereas Stein Rokkan drew attention to the more formal "interaction between external and internal boundary-building strategies" (Rokkan 1974:49). This interplay between external and internal control forces is, in this context, most interesting from an analytical point of view, as it is here we may find explanations why the explicit policies often do not work in practice.

Apart from the internal interaction between state policies and the various societal forces, there is, as the former discussion has indicated, also an interaction between states internationally. There is usually a close connection between the national politics and the dynamics of the international context, both in terms of general migration pressure and connected to other states' immigration policies. Concentrating on the national scene, this last intersection will, however, not be target for analysis here.

Both the internal and the external control formation may be seen as continua. For the sake of clarity, each formation will be divided into an *explicit* and an *implicit* dimension: *Explicit* meaning official policy, and *implicit* meaning hidden or subdued control mechanisms, and more or less systematic malpractice of official policies. The explicit dimension is by definition *open*, whereas the implicit dimension might be concealed or might occasionally have explicit or public expressions. Again, the distinctions are not clear cut. There exist grey areas in-between the boxes (Figure 5), as well as important interactions across the spheres.

Explicit control
The external explicit control is most easily identified and legitimized in the context of nation-states. The boundaries of the state defines, as we have seen, the group belonging to the

Figure 5. External–internal boundary building

	Implicit	Explicit
External	– Erratic handling of entry restrictions / elements of arbitrariness – Indistinct definitions of 'needs of the nation' – Redefinitions related to refugees	– Entry restrictions / border control – Visa schemes – Penalties for carrying companies – Computerized data bases on 'unwanted persons' – Development aid
Internal	– Hostility; marginalisation and social exclusion – General social control	– Internal surveillance – Access to ID-cards – Divergent accesses to living facilities, social benefits etc. – Employer sanctions – Union Policies – 'Amnesties' – Citizenship

state. Historically, it has been the sovereign right of the state to control entry into its territory.

However, this highly simplistic external control concept has to be refined and extended in the context of modern states – due to the changes in the international migration complex. As discussed earlier, efforts to achieve a manageable *and* minimal influx into Western Europe since the early 1970s have brought about substantial changes in the migration patterns. Since entries legitimized on humanitarian grounds have opened up new avenues for disadvantaged persons, and since repressing illegal entry is hard, receiving states have increasingly seen the need for new instruments in the external control system. Visa schemes,[69] penalties for carrying companies, computerized databases on "unwanted persons" etc. have been introduced as control mechanisms. Even development aid – aimed at reducing emigration from pressure areas by addressing the "root causes" – may be seen as a form of long-distance external control.

Internal explicit control has developed partly as a consequence of the imperfections of external control. Immigrants who have managed to gain entry to the territory illegally can be detected internally and treated according to the rules. Since there is also the possibility of entering a country *legally* (as a tourist, student, seasonal worker, etc.) internal surveillance is also a method for catching "overstayers" – those who fail to leave the country when their permits expire.

There are also explicit internal mechanisms that can be seen more as a part of the general national regulation system. Control of access to various facilities – ID-cards, housing, schooling, social benefits, etc. – means that irregular foreigners can be located. These mechanisms do not *obstruct* illegal sojourn, but they make life as an illegal resident in an advanced state more difficult.

---

69. There is currently a tendency that visa policy and asylum policy are connected in the sense that receiving states impose visa requirements on citizens from states generating refugees.

Sanctions against employers are both a preventive and a remedial means for attacking illegal employment – a means also targeted at irregular employment of *nationals*.

Union policies can have both a direct and an indirect impact on aliens control. With varying force, unions may serve as a "structural police" against social dumping caused by irregular work undertaken by natives or by foreigners. In Scandinavia where unions traditionally have represented a considerable political force, this "police function" has been quite marked. Immigrant workers thus tend to find work in branches where union influence is weak, like certain sections of the service sector (catering and domestic work). Unions may in some societies, due to their central role in the corporative state, also play a more general role in terms of securing higher standards as to working conditions and living conditions. Unions may therefore support a generous line towards foreigners (when these are registered as residents) to avoid the creation of a systemic "under-class".

National labour unions thus find themselves in a dilemma where their interests will often direct them to maintain a restrictive line on *entry*, but a generous/integral attitude towards legal foreign residents. For this reason, regularization ("amnesties") is a policy often favoured by unions.

Amnesties have increasingly become an internal control mechanism, particularly in Southern Europe where illegal entries represent a considerable problem. Illegals are invited to register and become legals, consequently becoming subject to official regulations of various kinds.

The ultimate explicit internal control mechanism is the option of naturalization, of gaining full citizenship. This innermost and sometimes most attractive gate represents the formal and symbolic cutting edge between life as a "foreigner" and life as a "national". It embodies the moment when one leaves the statistics of aliens and (at least ideally) escapes aliens control.

A relevant question is whether there are causal connections between the kind of external control practised and the way internal control is undertaken. Is, for example, lax external control combined with strict internal control (in an explicit sense)? One might argue that Great Britain has practised quite strict external control over the past 10–20 years, whereas its internal control has been more lax. Italy, on the other hand, until 1982 put strongest emphasis on the internal control (Sciortino 1991). In Scandinavia, Sweden has (at least in the past), been characterised by fairly permissive external scrutiny in terms of more liberal entry restrictions, whereas its internal supervision has been systematically organized through public control mechanisms, like tax systems and computerized population registers.[70] In France, between 1950 and 1972, illegal immigration was, according to the official view, a major benefit to the French economy, contributing to rapid growth and enhanced living conditions. French policy during this period was accordingly to allow relatively open borders, while restricting access to welfare benefits and keeping a generally strict internal control (Withol de Wenden 1990).[71] In the political process related to the Schengen Agreement as well as the turbulence around the elimination of border controls within the Internal Market, the linkage between external and internal control has also been in the forefront. Claims concerning "compensatory measures" for relaxing border controls are in essence a demand for tighter internal control measures.

Implicit control
The focus on control has, as we have seen, both real and symbolic significance. When immigration pressure is on the increase, it is pertinent to retain influx control to maintain state regulation of markets and the ability to plan. This becomes especially important in times of economic recession. It is also symbolically important for governments to appear to have

---

70. All residents in Scandinavia have a personal identification number that is required when, e.g. visiting a doctor or a hospital, when registering children in school etc.
71. Immigrants who were caught breaking the law or offending "ordre public" could be arbitrarily deported (ibid.)

control of their borders.[72] The population must have confidence that protection against uncontrollable influxes is effective, otherwise the climate for tolerance will deteriorate, and the government's capability will be called into question. This has been a rising problem as the gap between official (closed door) policies and *de facto* increases in immigrant communities has widened since the 1970s.

The large numbers of illegal immigrants found particularly in certain EU countries point up this problem. As mentioned, some sectors of the economies cannot manage without foreign labour (cheap labour).[73] However, the problem is that it is *illegal*, and therefore generates anti-immigrant feelings, and may render the government seem incapable of controlling borders.

On top of these subtleties, erratic or inefficient border control belongs to the implicit sphere. Despite laws and regulations, a considerable number of people will manage to enter due to inconsistent handling of restrictions and a certain degree of arbitrariness. Apart from the unintentional inefficiencies there will, in liberal democratic states, always be weak spots due to the humanitarian values held by these states.

Another implicit (and perhaps explicit) external control precept that has recently been presented by Western authorities, is the redefinitions related to refugees. The new notion of "safe countries"[74] adds a collective dimension to what used to be individual refugee protection – a notion that has clearly been introduced for control purposes. The related meaning of "economic refugee" is similarly an attempt to delimit the refugee concept, and establish legitimacy for further restrictions.

The implicit *internal* control pertains to the *clôture sociale* – the invisible social barriers that often present themselves in terms of lack of access rather than offensive prohibitions. Foreigners are

---

72. It is argued that public opinion is more sensitive to the *impression* of control that to the actual exercise of control (Withol de Wenden 1990).
73. Besides, it is necessary to keep the borders relatively open for tourists, businessmen, students, etc., as we have seen.
74. This notion implies that any asylum seeker can be returned to the first "safe" country he or she has passed through on the way.

often made to feel that they do not *belong*, and therefore cannot take part, through subtle mechanisms that need not be explicitly hostile. These non-formal control mechanisms can, of course, also be more openly and at times systematically unfriendly and excluding. In addition, more or less systematic discrimination and marginalization belong in this domain.

Another internal control mechanism of relevance, basically towards legally resident foreigners, is the implicit control that follows from attachment to and dependency on welfare provisions. The structural paternalism epitomized in the welfare state does have social control as a side effect.[75] These mechanisms have probably been most discernable among asylum seekers and refugees who are dependent on special assistance upon arrival. Often they remain in a client situation, either because they are not allowed to work or they are not capable of finding a job. This "clientalization" or generation of dependence can also be seen among legal foreign residents who for various reasons may have greater problems than the average national in finding appropriate work or adjusting to local conditions. Social exclusion and marginalization represent *processes* that are often self-reinforcing and therefore hard to reverse. As to the connections between the implicit external and internal control, we have already indicated that it is important for the state to appear to have control of its borders. If the population does not trust the state in this respect, social closure might be a consequence.[76] If there is erratic handling of entry restrictions or unforeseen consequences of entry control policy with new and/or unexpected categories of migrants appearing, hostile and excluding attitudes towards *all* foreigners may develop. These attitudes may be directed generally towards foreigners independent of their status as residents. The heavy emphasis on immigration *con-*

75. See Ian Culpitt (1992) for a general discussion on the welfare state and control mechanisms.
76. This internal mechanism is also attached to the external *explicit* control, as we previously saw through the example of Michael Walzer's statement.

trol since the 1970s, combined with the subsequent increase in asylum seekers as well as illegal immigrants, has made it difficult to avoid a rising stigmatization of immigrants in society. The immigration "stop" was meant to put an end to new ethnically "visible" immigrants, apart from a very few traditional *bona fide* refugees as well as family members of established migrants. "Immigrant" thus became synonymous with "unwanted", a fact that feeds back into attitudes towards legitimately integrated immigrants. Public opinion has become "confused" as to who is who. This public ambiguity is illustrated by the "amnesties" in Southern Europe: They are not wanted in the first place, and yet, once they have managed to get in, they may gain legal status. Aside from the signals these "regularisations" send to potential regions of *emigration*, what they communicate to citizens of the receiving country is quite double-edged: The authorities are "asserting the right to stay for the already-established immigrant, while identifying the new immigrant as a potential danger" (Sciortino 1991:93).

To fully trace the various control mechanisms at work in a given country is a complex endeavour, as it involves analysing complicated social processes not always openly linked to the migration complex. The notion of "general social control" is unwieldy in itself, as is its causal connection to the migration question. The interaction between the explicit policy and the more subtle mechanisms is also difficult to trace empirically.

The network dimension
So far the control complex has been analysed from "above": which factors and forces interplay explicitly and implicitly in the area of immigration control, and which factors serve to undermine or weaken the intended policy of the authorities. There is, however, also a "migratory counter-complex" that seems to be as important as the fallacies and contradictions discussed so far, in explaining changing migratory patterns and tendencies. This concerns the network dimension in migration systems.

Potential migrants do not respond to reality like "atomistic flies", as Robin Cohen (1987) puts it. There are multi-faceted networks established over the years between sender and receiver countries, involving various institutions (kinship groups, villages, recruitment agencies, companies, employers' associations, etc.). These networks act to channel (directly or indirectly) migrants to specific destinations. The presence of large communities of foreigners in some European countries may serve as a promoter to migration in the first place. Such networks may act as *buffers* or mediators between the individual immigrant and the internal control structures in the receiving country. The scope of the networks' field of operations is likely to be related to the internal control formation; where there is extensive structural control, the networks' abilities will be more limited. And conversely, in countries where the entry of large groups of foreigners has been allowed (or made possible), and the control of the labour market is more lax, the networks may play an extensive role in work intermediation, making it easier for the individual new migrant. Networks also seem to *stabilize* migration flows when established. As Portes and Kelly point out, the dynamics of social networks explain why migration flows often act differently from what is anticipated by conventional economic theory (1989:21).

Thus, the existence of migratory networks makes counter-strategies possible for migrants. Networks can provide "escape routes" in concrete pressed situations, and they can more systematically encourage circumvention of the control policies of receiving countries. This is similar to what Anthony Giddens (1985) calls "the dialectics of control in social systems", as we saw in the introductory chapter. According to such dialectics, all strategies of control call forth counter-strategies on the part of the subordinates, which in essence implies that even the weakest actor will hold some power in relation to the superordinate. The counter-strategies in this context may entail highly organized networks on both the sending and receiving side of the migratory bridge, and with networks even being "professionalized" with huge sums of money involved. On the other hand, network strategies may also be small in scope, perhaps involving only a few individuals, and having an informal organization.

The presence of strategic networks may serve as a "multiplier" in the migration system, promoting new contingents of illegal (and legal) immigrants, provided "holes" can be found in the external fence. Networks therefore become a central part of the total "pull package" for potential immigrants. And conversely: when networks are not present, possibly as a consequence of a strict internal (and/or external) control system, the attraction is accordingly weaker. If a society, therefore, has a reputation internationally of being highly controlled (in various forms) internally, the state might not have to police its borders in the first place.

These added effects and self-reinforcing mechanisms may partly explain why in a relatively homogeneous region like Western Europe there are striking contrasts in number of applications for asylum,[77] candidates for family reunion, as well as illegal entries.

The external/internal immigration control system of a country is basically formulated to select and restrict inflows, and to uphold law and order according to the overall immigration policy. In today's Western Europe, the dominating order in this respect is negatively defined: how to keep the migratory masses outside the borders. The *positive* side of immigration policies in contemporary Western Europe is the integration policy – the policy that applies to the ones who have managed to get a legal residency.

---

77. In 1992, the peak year so far, Germany received nearly 440,000 asylum applications, more than all the other EU countries taken together (*Migration News Sheet*, January 1993). The discrepancy between Germany and the other European countries has thus been growing the last few years. UNHCR figures reveal that between 1983 and 1991 more than 2,2 million asylum seekers were received in the 18 countries that report to UNHCR. More than 70% of all requests were submitted in EU countries (figures referred in Hovy 1992). Since German authorities introduced the new and more restrictive asylum law in June 1993 the numbers have, however, fallen by approximately 70% (*Migration News Sheet* 1 May 1994).

Chapter 6

Integration of Immigrants

There are important connections between immigration and integration – or more precisely between entry regulation and immigration/integration policies, yet it took (as observed by Hammar (ed.) 1985:273) strikingly long time to understand the importance of this interplay. This interplay is complex and there is no simple causal relationship. Both entry regulation and integration policies will always be affected by a whole range of other factors as well.

The very concept of "integration" has stimulated a complex debate.[78] In sociology, it refers to "the principles by which individuals or actors are related to one another in a society" (Marshall (ed.) 1994). There is, however, no assumption that the relationships described in this definition are harmonious: social integration can include both harmony and conflict. Nevertheless, in the context of immigration, the idea of integration is introduced to *avoid* conflict.

So far, the conception of "integration" in relation to immigrants has relied heavily on the "theoretical imagery of assimilation"[79] (Portes and Böröcz 1989), understood as a unilin-

---

78. Etienne Balibar is provoked by the implicit notion of "them" versus "us" in this debate. He finds it peculiar to talk in terms of *integrating* "people who have been an integral part of the social structure of our countries for one, two or even three generations" (Silverman (ed.) 1991:82).
79. Assimilation literally means "making similar".

ear process of immigrant adaptation to the recipient society. Minority groups adopt the cultural norms and lifestyles of the new society, by renouncing their original cultural attachments. According to this theory, in the end immigrant minorities will logically disappear, blending into society as a whole. Assimilation theory is related to the general functionalist tradition in sociology, with assimilation being the end result of a process marked by diminishing social disequilibrium initially created by conflicting cultural values and norms. The pace of adaptation will vary, yet the elements of the process, which is believed to be irreversible, are basically the same (ibid.)

Although this simplistic theory of assimilation has not endured the confrontation with reality, elements of the *thinking* still persist. The difference between "integration" and "assimilation" is basically a question of orientation; which elements one stresses most. Recent European history has shown that this emphasis is variable in the sense that changing government or general political climate entail redefinitions of the concepts. "Integration" has vaguely come to mean equality in basic rights and duties, yet without pressure to conform culturally.

The definition exercise is taking place in a continuous interplay with other central forces in society. Immigration is always a part of a wider social and national process, just as the perception of immigration always is a part of this process. Immigration indirectly turns the focus to the native population – their history, traditions, political values, self-reflection and identity.

Integration policy can only be understood on the basis of specific characteristics of the populations involved, which basically presupposes a certain acknowledgement of cultural and ethnic plurality.

Integration must be a dialogue between two arenas: the formal official system in terms of rules and activities, and the informal processes which are partly invisible, yet nevertheless essential for the process of integration.

Ideally, social integration is a result of *interaction* – and *com-*

munication. Integration should not imply that one part gives up his or her own cultural luggage, and dissolves into something foreign. Neither does it mean that the individual remains isolated in her/his own tradition.

A necessary condition for communication leading to integration is that difference is tolerated. A successful communication process requires that representatives of the receiving society are able to see themselves from outside: What are the peculiarities of their own culture, and how are others likely to react?

A basic supposition here is that "culture"[80] is not a static thing. It provides premises as well as products of social processes, and it changes in confrontation with other "cultures"; and these confrontations make the contrasts more visible. Integration means changing all the involved parts – a process that develops through creating something new.

In official documents and in "common knowledge" a "functional" concept of integration is usually applied. By and large, this means "immigrants' adaptation to the institutions, norms and culture of the «majority society» to the extent necessary for the group's members to function in the society while at the same time keeping intact its own ethnic identity" (Ålund and Schierup (eds.) 1991:14). In other words, adaptation to the already defined functional demands of established institutions and organizations.

Control and integration

France in the late 1960s and early 1970s witnessed what Silverman (1990) has labelled a policy aimed at creating "a new

---

80. The concept "culture" has been subject to much debate lately. At a conference in 1990 the Norwegian anthropologist Fredrik Barth ironically suggested that the scientific community should abstain from the term for six months as a test to whether it was possible to live without it (referred in Hylland Eriksen 1991). A useful distinction could nevertheless be that "culture" is the constantly changing "common meaning" that is established when people act together: Culture is an aspect of social relations, yet it does not give any detailed prescriptions as to how the individual should act (ibid.).

consensus". From a nearly *laissez faire* policy on immigration, letting in people according to the market forces, the early 1970s introduced a new approach: immigration was increasingly seen as a social problem which called for stricter regulation. New measures were introduced (through, e.g. the so-called Marcellin-Fontanet circulars) in 1972. Firstly, these aimed at curbing the system of regularization (amnesties), where unofficial immigrants could legalize their position by giving evidence of employment. Secondly, the state agency ONI (*Office National d'Immigration*) was reinstated, as the major regulator of entry into the country. The 1972 circulars made the linkage between work and stay more direct: entry and residence were made dependent on evidence of work and a formal work permit. Failure to fulfil these criteria was to result in expulsion (Silverman 1990).

These attempts to control immigration also had a considerable ethnic component. ONI was to institute what Silverman calls a "racialized two-tier system of immigration", whereby Europeans were stimulated to settle permanently, whereas non-Europeans were seen as temporary immigrants.

This tougher stand on immigration from non-OECD countries must (in France as elsewhere in Western Europe) be placed in its historical context. As we have seen (Chapter 2) the question of social cohesion in the wake of extensive 1960s immigrant settlement, had appeared on the political agenda. This left the authorities in a dilemma which resulted in the "two-tier policy": fears of social unrest due to "ethnic imbalance" favoured restrictions on non-OECD immigration; at the same time the continued demand for (certain types of) manpower implied the encouragement of particularly European immigration. The economic argument for curtailing immigration of low-skilled manpower reinforced this picture later in the 1970s.

Even though a structural connection between the labour market and entry control was intentionally established with the new restrictive regulations, still the authorities had to approach what was believed to be ethnically based tension and unrest. This is the background for the introduction of a complementary policy aimed at integrating those immigrants who were already legitimately established. This "double strategy" was apparently first introduced in France (see Silverman 1992), but soon set the tone in many other Western European countries.

A *causal* argument has been pursued for this strategy. A successful integration policy is said to *depend* on strict entry control. Free influx of aliens was seen as the major obstacle as to the establishment of a peaceful relationship between immigrant and national communities.

This "double strategy" reflects both *realpolitik* and *rhetoric*. Free immigration *can* be a threat to society because it can undermine state regulation of labour and housing markets and make planning virtually impossible. It may also eventually alter the preconditions for welfare states like those built up in Western Europe after World War II.

The rhetorical aspects of the strategy concerns the "moral compromise" which is contained in it. Declarations of intention to integrate immigrants serve to *legitimate* a stricter control.[81]

The authorities often declare that restricting immigration is a move to benefit already established immigrants, and a necessary precondition for easing inter-ethnic relations. Just what is in the interest of the already admitted immigrants is, however, not an easy question. Legal immigrants would at least have an interest in liberal family reunion arrangements as well as possibilities of having friends and more distant relatives visit. For newcomers the existence of established immigrant networks is of great importance to ease the introduction to the new society. It can also be argued that a restrictive entry policy may influence people's *general* attitudes towards immigrants. We can note tendencies in Europe today to the effect that long-term residents and even naturalized immigrants face increasing

---

81. Here we have a parallel in the asylum debate: Leniency towards asylum seekers is said to make the situation worse for "real" refugees.

hostility and discrimination (see, e.g. Wilpert 1991). This may however, also be a result of the confusion as to "who is who" among the immigrants, as mentioned above.

On the other hand, established immigrants may gain a more stable living and working situation if the flow of newcomers is restricted. There is empirical evidence that in segmented labour markets, fresh immigration tends to squeeze out immigrants from former waves, rather than native workers. Pressure on the housing market is also relevant here.[82] Consequently, it might be argued that lack of/insufficient entry restrictions may deteriorate the situation for *all* immigrants.[83]

Policy measures aimed at integration

"All governments are becoming aware of the urgent need for ambitious policies in this [integration of immigrants]. But while the diagnosis may be the same in all countries, the attention given to the problem and the resources allocated for tackling it are not always commensurate with the needs identified" (Commission 1992b:9). This statement in a Commission Working Document from 1992 could stand as a general comment concerning integration measures in most Western European countries since the introduction of the "double strategy" in the early 1970s. Moreover, approaches have differed from country to country, for historical and political reasons.

A distinction is usually made between *direct* and *indirect* measures. "Direct" immigration policy means official schemes and activities targeted specifically at immigrants – language training, housing schemes, information services, etc. "Indi-

---

82. Rainer Bauböck, unpublished paper 1993.
83. An opinion survey in France undertaken by the Sofres Institute revealed that a majority of immigrants were in favour of the new and more restrictive French immigration laws – with the exception of the new conditions concerning family reunification. A majority (57%) also favoured stricter control of asylum seekers (*Migration News Sheet*, August 1993:3).

rect" immigration policy means general or universalistic measures intended to entail all legal residents. Whereas the in-direct immigration policy indicates a state's general social ideology, direct immigration measures also reflect its general immigration policy (Hammar (ed.) 1985). The emphasis on direct as opposed to indirect measures varies, but nearly all countries in Western Europe have elements of both. Direct measures have developed as a reaction to the post-1970s' real-ization that immigration tends to be permanent, and that some sort of "positive discrimination" is a necessary interme-diate instrument to ease integration. The specific measures in this respect tend to be highly controversial, sometimes chal-lenging the popular support for welfare state values. Never-theless, the question of direct measures towards immigrants is related to the assimilation/integration complex. Should immi-grants be stimulated to become "French", "German", or "Bel-gian" as soon as possible, or should the preservation of origi-nal language and culture be allowed, or indeed, encouraged?

Lack of dedication to direct policies aimed at integrating im-migrants can sometimes be legitimized in a positive way. France has long held that integration should be a "natural" result of living in French culture, and should consequently not be pursued through direct governmental measures.[84] This approach, subsequently modified somewhat, is heritage of the universalistic *égalité* principle of the French Revolution: to promote a society where all individuals are free and equal. The "making of equality" in relation to immigrants is to be pur-sued through gradual assimilation. The school system has been strategic in this respect. Through education every child is to be adopted into French society and culture. Throughout the years, French authorities have had success on their own prem-ises. Several former immigrant groups have indeed become "French" in most meanings of the term. For instance, Italians

---

84. Equally, the British government long resisted direct intervention to accom-modate immigrants, referring to the discriminatory aspects of such measures (Layton-Henry 1984).

and Poles who arrived before World War II are today, for all practical purposes, indistinguishable from other French citizens. However, immigrants who arrived later have had greater difficulties, or have resisted this merger more vigorously – like postwar immigrants from Portugal, and not least North Africans (Stalker 1994).

Even Germany, which for so long has insisted that it is not "an immigration country", has realized that certain immigrant groups in fact have come to stay, and that the government consequently has to work out specific programmes aimed at integration. This applies mainly to migrant workers from the Mediterranean countries and their families, and Germany's programmes are primarily targeted at the second and third generation of this immigrant group (Mehrländer 1994). This direction in German alien policy is, however, not meant to indicate that Germany is willing to define itself as an immigration country. According to Ursula Mehrländer, the government sees this as a unique historical experience which should not be repeated. These integration measures coincide with reinforced attempts to limit any further influx of alien groups (ibid.:8–9).

Diverse categories of migrants: Implications for integration

Immigration control can, as we have seen, be spelled out differently in relation to the various migrant categories. This is definitely also the case with the question of integration.[85]

Immigrant workers
This category, which constituted the bulk of immigrants in Western Europe before the early 1970s, has in recent years been expanded to include various arrangements, at the same

---

85. A similar categorization related to *territorial status* is made in Rainer Bauböck, unpublished paper (1993).

time as regular labour immigration is intentionally reduced to a minimum through the prolonged "immigration stop" policy. As we have seen, demand for specific kinds of labour has made some of the EU countries open up for temporary and restricted recruitment programmes: frontier workers, seasonal labour, contract workers, etc. These categories are not included in policies aimed at integration. Quite the opposite, in fact. The lesson of the post-1970s has taught the authorities of these countries to avoid integration through protracted settlement. The new labour arrangements are designed to be only short-term – with enforced return once the work contract expires.

On the other hand there are the former "guest workers" who became settlers. They constitute a group that is, or has become, integrated one way or another. These long-term foreign workers are also a diverse group between and within the various EU countries. The legal benefits to which they are entitled vary according to different dimensions: period of residence; skills/career; citizenship of origin etc. Among EU countries, policies towards immigration in general are important in this respect. Germany with its insistence on not being an immigration country would naturally be less inclined to institute measures aimed at integration than, e.g. the Netherlands, with its colonial history and more developed "denizen approach" (see Chapter 1). Foreigners without denizen status have less secure residence rights and are more vulnerable to fluctuations in the economy. This in turn makes conditions for integration more restrained.

Illegal immigrants and irregular foreign workers
Obviously, illegal immigrants are deprived of the rights conveyed by regular resident permits and citizenship in welfare states. This situation varies, however; currently there is much debate as to which basic human rights ought to apply – health facilities, schooling for children, etc. It has recently also been questioned whether persons who enter a country without valid necessary documents should be made subject to asylum procedures on a regular basis. As noted, illegal immigrants

represent a large and apparently growing group in the various EU countries, often living an unstable existence at the margins of society. And yet, illegal immigrants may also stay for years in their niche of the labour market, once they have found out how to get around in society.

The question of integration in relation to illegal immigrants has a formal and a substantive side. Lack of access to public provisions like social security, services, and other benefits represent limitations as to their formal integration into the nation-state. On the other hand, irregular immigrant labour may be *de facto* fairly well integrated in their own niche of society, through work and neighbour relations – indeed, perhaps more so than accepted refugees or asylum seekers who may have to remain in reception centres for an extended period.[86] Regardless, it is logical that advanced welfare states in alliance with labour unions should consider illegal labour (whether foreign or national) un-integrated or integrated in ways deemed detrimental to society. Consequently, as long as states do not succeed in curbing illegal immigration and employment of irregular labour, regularizations or amnesties may, for both normative and practical reasons, represent occasional remedies. Too frequent amnesties may, on the other hand, serve to encourage further immigration.

Illegal foreign labour can also be said to be recruited on account of its status as cheap labour. Thus, its attraction lies at least indirectly in the very fact of illegality. Regularization of this labour may consequently worsen their immediate position in the market, and would therefore not be considered worth while.

Refugees and asylum seekers
According to the international migration discourse, a refugee is a person who enters a foreign country for different reasons than an immigrant. A refugee is in principal victim of political vio-

---

86. According to Claude-Valentin Marie (1991) the growth in private-sector employment of immigrants (legal and illegal) in France is an indication of adaptability and eventually some sort of integration.

lence or persecution, whereas an immigrant moves for economic or other reasons (family reunion, education, etc.) In recent years another distinction, attached to the arrangement through which refugees arrive, has become important. A refugee may arrive organized by either the receiving country or through an international agent like UNHCR; asylum seekers may arrive "spontaneously", basically on their own initiative. The refugees under UNHCR protection (often termed "quota refugees") have their status decided beforehand, whereas asylum seekers risk being turned down in the country of arrival. Recently a third category – "war refugees" – has gained significance in the wake of the crisis in former Yugoslavia. When these war-refugees are accepted, they are granted *temporary residence* including certain welfare provisions, even though their status might not be based on the Geneva Refugee Convention.

These distinctions have had important implications for reception facilities and for the efforts by the authorities to accommodate and perhaps integrate the various groups. Among the three groups (and immigrants from non-OECD countries in general), Convention refugees enjoy a fairly privileged position. Their right of residence is secured until the political situation improves in their home country, they receive significant resettlement assistance, they are entitled to social services and rights on equal terms with citizens, and they are permitted to work. All this does not guarantee a successful economic integration, however; in fact, it may lead to prolonged dependence on public assistance. Yet the facilities represent an asset in the early adaptation period, which none of the other immigrant categories enjoy (Portes and Böröcz 1989). After asylum seekers became a significant and growing group among international refugees, separate and restrictive rules have successively been instituted in the various recipient countries.[87] Sometimes asylum seekers are not allowed to work while their case

---

87. Despite the convergence of political practice in relation to this group in recent years in Western Europe (e.g. reflected in the Dublin Convention), there is still variation among receiving countries as to specific arrangements for asylum seekers.

is being investigated;[88] allowances have been shrinking, they are now frequently delivered in kind, and the standard of accommodation has deteriorated.

Individual variables
For the individual migrant, the category assigned to him or her will be important in relation to integration. Additionally, individual background variables will in each case contribute in determining how the integration process proceeds. I have in another context (Brochmann 1993) structured these individual variables into three clusters: 1)initial resources; 2) process conditions; 3) cumulative results. In our context, the first cluster would include class background, education/training, general resources in terms of former participation/organizational experience, political practice, possible traumatic experiences, conditions of exit, etc. The second cluster would designate conditions around reception and consequently assignment to one of the three main categories of migrants, early experiences in the new country including (official and other) facilities available, access to assistance, contacts with immigrant networks, contact with the local population, etc. The third cluster would here signify the interplay between these individual socio-economic and psychological qualities and experiences on the one hand, and the concrete conditions immigrants are confronted with in the receiving societies on the other. The complex meeting between individual immigrants and the receiving society will be conditioned by these diverse and interconnected processes.

The time dimension

The time dimension is important, both in terms of the migrants' own mental filters, and of official approach in the receiving countries.

---

88. Different countries have moved back and forth on this issue, partly contingent on labour market needs. Currently, asylum seekers under investigation are allowed employment in Germany; since 1991, this has not been the case in France.

The "guest workers" of the 1960s and 1970s were by definition seen as temporary labour, meant to leave after an inten-
sive work period, or to commute according to fluctuations in
the market. Consequently no efforts were made to integrate
them into society. After the recruitment stop in the mid 1970s,
and the gradual recognition of the fact that "the guests had
come to stay" (Rogers 1985), the authorities have had to face
the question of integration. This has been done with various
intensity, yet most countries have at least followed a policy al-
lowing family reunification. The different *contract* workers of
today are not subject to any integration mechanisms. Quite
the opposite: the limited duration (and other mechanisms)
have been instituted to avoid settlement and integration.

Illegal labour represent a complex group, ranging from the
deliberate "hit-and-run" migrants who may travel in and out
according to demand in their niche in the labour market, to
people who actually stay on for years and who psychologically
may feel "integrated" into their part of society although they
have never been reached by any public scheme. Time is also an
important factor in relation to the regularizations/amnesties
occasionally offered the illegal workers; to become legalized,
one normally has to document a work relation for a specifically defined period.

For accepted refugees, features like permanent residence,
social provisions and access to the labour market are signals
from the authorities that theirs can be a prolonged stay, which
again implicitly (and at times explicitly) opens the door to permanent settlement and integration in society. Various specific
efforts are made to facilitate this. Concerning asylum seekers,
the crucial point is, of course, the result of the investigation.
Ideally, from the perspective of view of the authorities, rejec-
tion should imply deportation. Although this is now practiced
to an increasing degree in many Western European countries,
still a much higher percentage of asylum seekers manage to
stay than what is implied by the figures of accepted applications. Time proves to be a key factor in determining whether a
non-accepted asylum seeker should be allowed to stay on "hu-

manitarian grounds". Time-consuming procedures have meant that asylum seekers often become mentally settled in their new country, and sometimes in fact also integrated in local communities.[89] Concerning the "war refugees" with "temporary protection" the question of integration poses a delicate dilemma for governments. It is seriously implied in the arrangement that repatriation should be effectuated when the situation allows it. Yet the time perspective is highly uncertain, which again works against *de facto* repatriation. On the other hand, if the sojourn is likely to last, then the integration issue should be taken seriously. In some countries it has also been argued that integration in recipient communities *facilitates* a smoother repatriation when the time is ripe.[90]

Repatriation and marginalization

There are, logically speaking, two consequences of non-integration of long-term immigrants: repatriation or marginalization. Both France and Germany have at times launched schemes to encourage *voluntary* repatriation of migrants, neither of which has proven very successful (see Silverman 1992; Mehrländer 1994). In the German case it is argued that the legislation designed to stimulate (through financial support) non-Germans to return to the place of origin, influenced only those who would have wanted to leave at any rate. Only a very small group took advantage of the scheme (Mehrländer 1994). Making repatriation public policy may also have some unforeseen consequences in terms of popular attitudes to-

---

89. In Norway there have been several cases where asylum seekers whose applications have been rejected, are vigorously protected by the local communities, in which they have been placed, when the authorities act to deport them.

90. This point is, e.g. stressed by the authorities in relation to Bosnians in Norway. It remains to be seen how this will function in practice. A similar attitude is reflected in the *Berliner Commission for Foreigners' Affairs* from 1985: "for many non-nationals, adherence to tradition represents a necessary component of the integration process. For only if one is secure in the knowledge that one's cultural identity is unchallenged can one have the inner self-assurance to open oneself up to an alien environment" (cited in Soysal 1993).

wards immigrants in general. It is hard to avoid the subtle message that non-nationals *should* "go home". This may on the one hand provoke hostility among nationals when repatriation fails to take place; it may, on the other hand, thwart immigrants' possibilities and motivation for integration when they choose to stay. *Involuntary* repatriation has so far not taken place to any significant degree from Western European countries. The test case here will arise with the refugees under "temporary protection", once the situation in former Yugoslavia is defined as "safe".

Marginalization of immigrants, although never publicly seen as a desirable option, is taking place throughout Europe: Immigrants have a higher unemployment rate than nationals in the same occupation, same age group, etc. (OECD 1995); they also have social problems in terms of lack of contact with the rest of society, lack of access to public arenas and facilities, limitations in participation and interaction politically and socially, etc. Marginalization can be a result of various kinds of discrimination, and/or of failing social competence to gain access. Either way, the marginalization of large groups of non-nationals serves as an indication of the shortcomings of integration policies. There is currently a growing opinion in all EU member-states that marginalization of immigrants carries heavy risks of social unrest and ethnic conflicts, particularly in times when also parts of the national population feel economic strains. As a consequence of this understanding, integration policies now rank higher on the agenda in EU countries.

We have in this chapter focused on the importance of structural/political and individual determinants in relation to the integration of immigrants. A central point has been the *interplay* between entry *control* and *integration*, substantially and rhetorically. A third dimension, the *labour market*, functions as a relatively independent force which implicitly (and partly explicitly) influences both control policy and efforts at integration.

Chapter 7

The Labour Market Dimension and the Welfare State

One might, like James Hollifield (1986), see the efficiency of immigration policy as one measure of the strength of the state. In modern welfare states this strength is more a question of the ability to supervise the labour market, than policing the national borders: it revolves on the state's ability to prevent employers from hiring undocumented workers and its ability to maintain generally high standards of employment conditions. The capacity to control inflows depends largely on how the labour market is organized and structured. In other words, the specific migration setting is the ongoing result of a combination of policy and market forces, so the control aspects discussed so far are constantly interplaying with labour market parameters as well as social forces attached to the blending process of cultures.

The labour market plays a decisive (although not all-embracing) role in the *integration* of immigrants. Absorption of the immigrant population in the regular labour force also disburdens public budgets and may contribute to economic growth. Both for the immigrants and for the national population the labour market can serve as a stepping stone for social integration.

Non-integration in the labour market, unemployment among immigrant workers and discrimination – these are themes that predominate in discussions on immigration and the labour market.

Table 10. Annual increase in the number of unemployed foreigners and total unemployed* in selected European OECD countries, 1987–91

		1987	1988	1989	1990	1991
Austria	Total	8.2	−3.5	−6.0	11.1	11.6
(ann. aver.)	Foreigners	14.8	−3.0	5.8	73.7	11.6
Belgium	Total	−1.5	−9.1	−9.6	−4.8	6.2
(end June)	Foreigners	−1.3	−3.5	−5.9	−1.8	6.1
France	Total	−1.5	−1.2	−2.3	1.0	11.8
(end Dec.)	Foreigners	−2.5	1.5	4.8	3.4	6.7
Germany**	Total	−	0.6	−9.1	−7.6	38.2
(ann. aver.)	Foreigners	5.7	2.8	−13.7	−12.7	9.3
Netherlands	Total	−1.2	−1.0	−7.7	−6.1	−
(end Dec.)	Foreigners	6.1	2.4	−0.7	−0.5	−
Sweden	Total	−27.9	−14.6	−14.5	12.9	76.0
(ann. aver.)	Foreigners	−8.7	−10.5	−3.5	24.4	64.7
Switzerland	Total	−3.7	−10.9	−22.5	5.6	119.4
(ann. aver.)	Foreigners	6.4	−6.3	−22.3	9.8	126.2

* National definitions of unemployment.
** As from 1991, data include Eastern part of Germany.

Ref.:   Austria: Bundesministerium für Arbeit und Soziales
    Belgium: Ministère de l'Emploi et du Travail
    France: Agence nationale pour l'emploi
    Germany: Bundesanstalt für Arbeit
    Netherlands: Centraal Bureau Voor de Statistiek, Buitenlandse wernemers,
      and from the 1.1.89, Bemiddelingbestand Zonder Baan
    Sweden: Statistics Sweden
    Switzerland: Office fédéral de l'industrie, des arts et métiers et du travail
Source: OECD (SOPEMI) Annual Report 1993

Nevertheless, it would be wrong to consider immigrants as a problem population in this respect: the *majority* of the immigrant population in Western Europe seems to be well integrated through the labour market (Commission 1992c).

The immigrant population has made a considerable contribution to the national economies through the creation of small and medium-sized enterprises, and through the growth

Table 11. Distribution of national, foreign and total employment between the eleven major industry divisions in 1991

Percentages

	0	10	20	30	40	50	60	70	80	90/1	90/2	Total
Belgium												
Nationals	2.8	1.4	4.2	8.5	9.5	5.8	17.1	7.7	8.3	10.6	24.1	100.0
Foreigners	1.0	0.7	10.3	12.7	9.4	12.6	22.9	5.0	6.5	1.8	17.2	100.0
Total	2.7	1.4	4.6	8.8	9.5	6.3	17.5	7.5	8.2	10.0	23.6	100.0
France												
Nationals	6.2	1.2	3.1	9.2	8.8	6.8	17.2	6.1	9.8	9.3	22.2	100.0
Foreigners	3.0	0.7	2.8	9.6	11.1	21.7	17.5	3.5	9.4	1.6	19.1	100.0
Total	6.0	1.2	3.1	9.3	8.9	7.6	17.3	6.0	9.7	8.9	22.1	100.0
Germany												
Nationals	3.7	1.6	4.9	15.8	9.5	6.7	16.6	5.8	8.8	9.1	17.5	100.0
Foreigners	1.2	1.8	7.5	26.6	13.4	7.7	16.8	4.5	4.0	1.6	14.8	100.0
Total	3.5	1.6	5.2	16.7	9.8	6.8	16.6	5.7	8.4	8.4	17.3	100.0
Luxembourg												
Nationals	4.5	1.4	9.3	2.7	7.5	4.3	18.5	8.6	13.5	13.4	16.3	100.0
Foreigners	1.3	0.7	5.0	4.8	6.2	19.9	23.1	3.6	12.0	2.0	21.3	100.0
Total	4.4	1.0	2.6	6.7	8.5	6.7	19.4	6.3	11.1	6.2	27.0	100.0

(Table 11, continued)

Percentages

	00	10	20	30	40	50	60	70	80	90/1	90/2	Total
Netherlands												
Nationals	4.5	1.0	2.5	6.6	8.4	6.8	19.3	6.3	11.2	6.3	27.1	100.0
Foreigners	1.4	1.7	4.9	12.1	12.1	3.7	22.3	6.5	7.6	3.4	24.1	100.0
Total	4.4	1.0	2.6	6.7	8.5	6.7	19.4	6.3	11.1	6.2	27.0	100.0
United Kingdom												
Nationals	2.4	2.2	3.2	9.8	8.7	7.5	20.3	6.3	11.4	6.6	21.6	100.0
Foreigners	0.5	1.0	2.6	8.3	7.8	7.3	21.4	5.6	10.7	4.4	30.2	100.0
Total	2.3	2.2	3.1	9.7	8.7	7.5	20.4	6.2	11.4	6.5	22.0	100.0

00   Agriculture, hunting, forestry and fishing
10   Energy and water
20   Extraction and processing of non-energy-producing minerals and derived products; chemical industry
30   Metal manufacture; mechanical, electrical, electronical and instrument engineering
40   Other manufacturing industries
50   Building and civil engineering
60   Distributive trades, hotels, catering, repairs
70   Transport and communications
80   Banking and finance, insurance, business service, renting
90/1   Public administration, national defence and compulsory social security; diplomatic representation, international organisations and allied armed forces
90/2   Other services
Source: Eurostat, Labour Force Survey, 1991, referred in OECD (SOPEMI) Annual Report 1993

in the number of independent workers among immigrants (OECD 1995).

When the "double strategy" replaced the "guest worker" orientation in the 1970s, there were also *positive* labour market considerations involved: Millions of foreigners occupied jobs that could not easily be replaced by others. The rotation principle of the immigrant labour force was, broadly speaking, not in the interest of most employers. Limited turnover implied stability and reduced costs in terms of recruitment and training; it improved labour relations and induced better production results. Immigrant labour had become indispensable in both the public and private sector, and the already-established workers were preferred to new replacements (Hammar 1985).

Effects on employment

The effect on employment is a crucial issue in relation to immigration, both in real terms and in relation to popular opinion. As we saw in Chapter 1, the cost-benefit calculations pertaining to immigration are highly complicated. Nevertheless, the fear that new immigrants will squeeze native workers out of their jobs is an underlying premise for much government policy in receiving countries. An implicit assumption in this respect is that the number of jobs in any country is basically fixed, and that an influx of excess labour will swamp the market. This is, according to Peter Stalker, a false picture: Immigration is only *one* way of increasing a country's population. Higher fertility rates or lower death rates are other ways. A population increase means more consumers of goods and services, more people whose needs have to be accommodated, and this may lead to the creation of more jobs. The specific situation will depend on, among other factors, how the economy works, and on the policies pursued by the government (Stalker 1994).

Orthodox liberal economic theory would regard immigrants as a *supplement* to national labour. According to this view, immigrant labour finds work in expanding economies when these have depleted national labour resources, resulting in labour shortage. Thus, the absorption of foreign labour into the lower strata of the labour market hierarchy is seen as an intrinsic consequence of an economic logic: Nationals climb toward better-paid and more prestigious jobs, whereas newcomers accept strenuous work on the bottom rungs of the ladder. Since labour shortages appear at the bottom, salaries for unskilled and semi-skilled labour tend to increase, due to competition among employers. Following this logic, employers would then look for new sources of labour in order to master inflation, and new streams of migrants would be attracted to the market opportunities. The result of this process is the perpetuation of immigration (Portes and Kelly 1989).

According to Portes and Kelly, this economic theory disregards the political motives that lead employers to hire foreign labour as a means to control domestic labour mobilization and demands. Immigration often coexists with considerable unemployment or underemployment of national workers; or immigrants are hired side by side with national workers "in order to neutralize claims for higher wages or better working conditions on the part of the domestic labour force" (ibid.:22).

The viewpoint that immigrants displace national workers equally supposes that the two groups are competing for the same jobs. Stalker argues that this is usually not the case, as immigrant workers tend to take jobs that nationals no longer want, like harvesting crops, unpleasant service work in, e.g. restaurants and hospitals, low-wage manufacturing or construction work, etc. (Stalker 1994).[91] Equally, a study by Gieseck, Heilemann and von Loeffelholz concludes that "the structural and demand side effects on the labour market re-

---

91. Hollifield argues that the high *visibility* of the work categories dominated by immigrants (primarily service functions like domestic service, various types of maintenance personnel, garbage collection, bus drivers, hospital work, etc.) contributes to the public xenophobia that immigrants are taking over jobs from national workers (Hollifield 1992:159).

sulting from immigration have apparently outweighed possible displacement effects" (Gieseck et al. (eds.) 1994:24).[92]

The "structural and demand side effect" is, according to a study undertaken by Massey et al., due partly to a "value shift" among national workers who reject "immigrant" jobs, making it necessary to retain or recruit more immigrants. Once immigrants have entered a job in considerable numbers, it gets labelled as a typical "immigrant job", and channelling native workers back into that occupational category becomes difficult. Consequently, along with domestic unemployment, governments find it infeasible to curtail labour migration and to recruit nationals back into jobs formerly held by immigrants (Massey et al. 1994:33). This argument is basically in line with the Marxist-inspired "dual labour market theory" of which the economist Michael Piore is probably the best-known proponent. According to Piore, the dual labour market hypothesis is "that the functioning of the labour markets is best understood in terms of a model in which the market is divided into a primary segment and a secondary segment. The jobs in the primary sector are largely reserved for natives. There is thus a fundamental dichotomy between the jobs of migrants and the jobs of natives, and the role of migrants in industrial economies can be traced to the factors that generate the distinction initially, to the role and function of the secondary sector in which migrants are found, and to the evolution of its labour requirements" (Piore 1979:35). Foreign workers are viewed as an essential element of labour supply in capitalist economies as they can be used as a flexible "reserve army" which is easy to hire and fire, apace with fluctuations in the economy. Consequently, immigrant labour enables firms to avoid "regulatory entanglements that govern the labour market in welfare states" (Hollifield 1992:7).

---

92. Studies from Australia conclude that migrants have had a relatively *neutral* effect on the labour market: immigrants have created as many jobs as they have occupied. These findings (referred in Stalker 1994:54), include the recession after 1984.

This dual labour market theory has been criticised from various angles. Primarily, it has been considered as having limited explanatory power as it focuses exclusively on the economy. Besides, other divisions than that between the primary and secondary labour market are said to be significant, as in the German case where the division between a temporary and a permanent labour market could be more analytically meaningful. Heisler also argues that while one may observe labour market segmentation in most advanced countries, the lines and the depth of the segmentation will vary (Heisler 1992: 632).

The second major employment consideration in relation to immigration concerns the wage depression argument. An influx of excess workers ready to take up work at comparatively low wages could reduce the general national wage level, it is argued, or could restrict wage increases. Without immigrant labour of this kind, wages for unpleasant jobs would have to be raised. This hypothetical argument is indeed difficult to refute. It seems to be a fact throughout Europe that immigrants, particularly the unskilled, earn lower wages than national workers, and that this wage difference persists over many years, although to a declining degree over time (Stalker 1994). However, the question is whether the absence of immigrants would cause wages to rise and subsequently entice national workers to do the unappealing work. Several scholars doubt that this would be the case (see Hollifield 1992; Stalker 1994; Piore 1979). Stalker points out that in all developed countries (including the newly industrialized economies in Asia), the dislike of strenuous manual labour is spreading as standards of education improve (Stalker 1994). Welfare state arrangements facilitate such avoidance reactions among national workers through unemployment benefits and the right to reject work below one's level of education/training or located outside the home vicinity. As Piore puts it, "the features that generate the unemployment – the instability, casual social relationships, unskilled work, and so on – are precisely those features that render the jobs unattractive to native workers."[93] This in turn implies that unemployment and immigration are linked only *indirectly* (Piore 1979:105). Taking in immigrants at the lower end of the wage scale does not *necessarily* reduce salaries for national workers. Stalker argues that instead it may increase their wage levels, through establishing or protecting the more highly skilled jobs for which national workers are more apt to apply (Stalker 1994). Besides, the widespread persistence of illegal immigration indicates a *de facto* demand which immigrant labour is meeting. Thus, the ethnically segmented labour market is partly a question of structural features of the economy, and is partly related to the control complex.

Illegal immigration – labour demand

The term "irregular/illegal immigrant worker" covers a whole range of categories: An immigrant worker may be "regular" in terms of residence but not in regard to work, or the other way around. There is the seasonal worker who moves to another sector in which he or she does not have a permit; then there is the temporary resident who has paid work but only a tourist visa; the legal temporary resident who stays on after the permit has expired; there is the regular student who works without a permit; the asylum seeker who works irregularly while the case is being examined and processed; the asylum seeker whose application has been turned down, yet who stays on, etc. (Commission 1992c). Even though such migrants are a highly vulnerable group in society, migrants also tend to be highly motivated economic actors, capable of following their own interests, including the urge to remain and work in the recipient country (Hollifield 1992:128).

The labour market plays a key role in relation to illegal immigration. An illegal worker implies an illegal employer – un-

---

93. Gary P. Freeman argues that immigrants to France before 1975 were recruited precisely for the purpose of filling the jobs at the bottom of the ladder; thus it was a question of a structurally embedded demand (Freeman 1979).

less the immigrant is provided for by close relatives or others. The size of illegal immigration depends to a large extent on how employers can utilize their labour. Access to work is a central attraction in relation to the establishment and maintenance of irregular immigration. Insofar as there exists work for these migrants when they arrive, the system will continue to function.

Irregular immigration was tolerated in some of the countries of the EC up till the 1970s. Since then the "irregulars" have become "illegals" or "clandestines". Nevertheless, the black labour market is dominated by *national* workers in every member country of the Community (Böhning and Werquin 1990).

An important lesson from the "amnesties" given to illegal immigrants in various places in Europe, is that it is impossible to control irregular immigration without attacking structural aspects of the labour market. Entry control, ID-checks, as well as various sanctions against employers and possible mediators can be only *a part of* a policy to curtail illegal immigration. Sanctions policies have been tried out in various countries. The overall experience is that sanctions must be effectuated with force and persistence to function. And they should be significant, to prevent fines from merely being calculated as a part of regular "business costs". Any *effective* sanctions policy is costly both in terms of finances and manpower (Papametriou 1991).[94]

The structural aspects of the labour market are complicated to come to grips with, indeed. The comprehensive presence of unauthorized immigrants indicates there are internal (unofficial) contradictions in the various receiving countries when it comes to the influx of cheap labour. Many people have an interest in illegal labour. Middle-class households are increasingly hiring domestics; the higher the official wage level, the

---

94. Employer sanctions are an old instrument, introduced in France as early as in 1926 and then again in 1946. Most European countries initiated this kind of sanction policy during the 1970s, not primarily in relation to illegal immigration, but as a means to control the labour market (Papametriou 1991).

greater is the temptation to do it "unofficially". There exist, among groups of employers within the various EU countries, several more or less open pressure groups concerning access to cheap foreign labour. Experiences from Italy reveal that restrictive legislation can co-exist with *de facto* lenience towards illegal labour in some contexts (Sciortino 1990). Variations between EU countries – in terms of labour market structure, size, and composition of the black labour market and hence variation in the patterns of the vested interests in foreign labour – are an important factor in the process towards harmonization of the European immigration policies.

The increase in illegal immigration has been an unforeseen consequence of the "immigration stop" introduced in the 1970s. The more complicated it becomes to enter Western Europe *legally*, the more illegal trafficking grows. Furthermore, the higher risks involved, the more lucrative is the business undertaken by traffickers. Irregular migration today represents a wide-ranging yet unwieldy terrain, where data are necessarily scarce and unreliable. The issue has become highly sensitive in the public debate, partly due to its magnitude (at least some places) and partly because of the discrepancy between the authorities' proclaimed continuous devotion to combatting the traffic, and their *de facto* incapacity/incapability to do so.

Irregular immigration in itself leads to insecurity and instability in the labour market, which again may mean greater difficulties for already resident immigrants to achieve integration into society. The "hidden economy" and irregular immigration tend to reinforce each other (see, e.g. Commission 1990),[95] in the sense that a continuous incentive exists to hire

---

95. The "black" labour market has grown in recent decades in many European countries. This is seen as a fact, even though figures are based on *estimations* – methods developed with varying degrees of sophistication throughout Europe. According to Marie (1987) clandestine immigration is seen as an important and rapidly advancing phenomenon particularly in Germany, Switzerland, France, Belgium, Italy, and Spain. Other investigations reveal that illegal immigration in some cases has meant a transfer of capital from the formal to the informal sector of the economy (Böhning and Werquin 1990).

illegally, since the supply is there. Sciortino argues that in Italy the basic reason behind ethnic tensions is the interaction between the various segments of the labour market – between the official and the shadow market. A concentration of illegal immigrants is encouraged where "semi-criminal labour brokering already operates, thus assuring the protection from the authorities" (Sciortino 1990:93). Thus the matching of cultural stereotypes and individual behaviour is mutually reinforcing through the labour market.

It can be argued that a similar relationship exists between the welfare state and the immigrants in areas where there are more asylum seekers than illegal immigrants. The "stop" has channelled immigrants into routes that are more costly for the authorities, and this in turn gives grounds for opinions that they come "to exploit our welfare state", resulting in increased hostility.

The welfare state dimension

James Hollifield (1992) argues that neither flexibility nor the reserve army function are relevant characteristics of the immigrant labour force in today's Europe. The Marxist assumption that foreign workers can function as dispensable commodities or buffers to be hired and fired according to trends in the labour market, does not hold water. Developments after the recession of the 1970s illustrate his point: immigration persisted and even sometimes increased, despite governmental policies aimed at exporting unemployment. According to Hollifield's theory of post-war migration, immigration to Europe (and the United States) can be understood only in the dual context of the spread of market relations domestically and internationally, as well as the ongoing extension of *rights* to non-citizen residents. Civil and social rights achieved by immigrants have established a span of protection for foreigners, which in turn makes repatriation or expulsion difficult (Hollifield 1992:165).

After World War II, the system of welfare states has lead to a major redefinition of social responsibility. Earlier, individuals had to rely on themselves or their immediate family for daily maintenance in times of trouble. With the welfare state, taxes made possible a redistributive system where social security became the responsibility of the state in most areas of society – in terms of sickness and unemployment benefits, old-age pensions, scholarships for education, etc. When public budgets are cut back, however, legitimacy becomes an issue: who should benefit and who should care for themselves. Then it becomes more explicit which *implicit* obligations society attaches to the "welfare contract". These are distinctly described (in the Norwegian case) by Hernes and Knudsen (1990): First and foremost, people should preferably take care of themselves. Secondly, those who have worked hard and contributed to the welfare budget all their lives, may legitimately take out old-age benefits when the time comes (and they should have priority if it is so that not everyone may benefit). Thirdly, all those who have been a part of the system (as well as their close relatives) should have the rights to benefit if needed.

The problem of solidarity towards poorly situated groups becomes particularly salient when newcomers arrive, people who have not "invested in society" over a life-time (let alone over generations). Two basic principles of the welfare state conflict in these matters: the value of humanitarian obligations is contested by an internal distributive logic. Generally speaking, this points to a central dilemma for Europe's welfare states today: The norms and values that define the democratic welfare state may be violated by excluding immigrants, either at the border or internally by not giving them access to social, economic, and political benefits. On the other hand, including them in the system could challenge people's sense of fairness when it comes to the divisions of burdens and rights among "those who struggled to construct the collective bargains represented by the welfare state" (Heisler and Heisler 1990).

This negative dynamic is more likely to be set in motion when resources become more limited; when an economic recession triggers off a collective insecurity in parts of the population.[96]

Indeed, this could be the core of the matter: The general crisis means marginalization and social exclusion even among the *native* population. Those who can still count themselves among the fortunate tend to protect their privileges, and build symbolic and real social barriers which may become ethnical or racial. And those who have fallen down and have become excluded transfer their agony to the newcomers (Wieviorka, 1992). The editor of *The Guardian*, Martin Woollacott, has put it very clearly: Anti-immigrant sentiments are "in essence a message of protest to the elites who have allowed traditions of national solidarity to slip and who have accommodated to the idea of a two tier society" (Woollacott 1992:35). "Die Biedermänner sind die Brandstifter" ("The men of honour are the incendiaries") it was equally claimed in an article on the situation in Germany (*Information* 2 July 1993). Security and belongingness are at stake internally, at the same time as international integration and dismantling of borders represent the imperative among the states of Western Europe.

Since regular labour migration is officially no longer wanted (apart from highly skilled labour in demand), a major part of the migration contingent is composed of immigrants legitimized on humanitarian grounds – asylum seekers/refugees and family members of earlier immigrants. Compared to the streams of workers from the 1960s and the early 1970s, these "new" migrants are primarily seen as a burden on the welfare budget.[97] They therefore mobilize the questions of justice mentioned above. On top of these humanitarian dilemmas with the trade-off between internal vs. external *solidarity*, there are important structural predicaments induced by com-

---

96. See Michel Wieviorka for an elaboration of structural reasons for racism and xenophobia in today's Europe (Wieviorka 1992).
97. Despite this common-sense perception of the cost-benefit status of post-1975 immigrants to Europe, more thorough calculations reveal a more complex picture (see among others Hollifield 1992; Freeman 1986).

prehensive immigration, whether it is motivated by economic or political forces.

Consequently, in political terms, immigration poses a notable challenge to the legitimacy of the modern welfare state. Real or perceived immigration pressure may lower the backing of those strata which used to constitute the major basis for welfare policies. The parallel process of increased immigration and the erosion of welfare-state provisions may start interacting, at least at the level of ideology and popular perceptions.

Ethnic division of labour and democracy

Illegal immigration represents the most obvious disturbance to any regulated labour market. On the other hand, access to work is a central attraction in relation to the establishment and the maintenance of irregular immigration, as we have seen.

Both labour unions and the state would have a clear interest in curbing illegal migration. Illegal labour represents a dumping problem, and it complicates economic planning. Certain employers, on the other hand, would individually profit from a sustained supply of cheap labour, as they can sidestep the normal social costs. Besides, it is argued, there are certain jobs that the indigenous work force no longer wants. The welfare-state system of social benefits facilitates this choosiness, even in periods of unemployment.

A possible dilemma for the welfare states in this context would be that the more regularizations ("amnesties") that are undertaken to incorporate illegals into the organized and controllable market, the higher become the incentives for new illegals to enter. The strength of this argument depends on labour market conditions in a wider context: whether there are alternative occupations in the legal part of the market. Otherwise, regularizations may not seem attractive enough for the illegals, as they may fear losing their jobs by registering. The main reason why they got their jobs in the first place was precisely that they were illegal and therefore "cheap".

Another dilemma for the states is the question of health provisions and even schooling facilities for the illegal worker and his/her family. On the one hand, social provisions should not act as another incentive mechanism – a magnet inducing more migration. On the other hand, lack of health care among marginalized groups could be a possible source of contagion; and exclusion from schooling could lead to the systematic creation of what in France is called a *classe dangereuse*, established with no other stable resources than social performance, organized villainy and drug trafficking (*Nouvel Observateur* no. 1479, 1993).[98] The message borne by this new class category is that illegal immigration not only represents a threat to economic and social standards in society, it also promotes lawlessness and disorder, which are indefensible in liberal democratic states. If, then, in order to deal with the problem, the state tries to connect aliens control with health and school provisions, immigrants may opt not to profit from the facilities, which would then lead the state back to square one.

If it is correct that democratic states do have the greatest problems in effective entry control, it is even more pertinent to control the *internal* situation, in other words to integrate immigrants into regular society and the labour market. If the democratic states do not succeed in this endeavour, they run the risk of having ethnic and social segmentation coincide in a lasting and systematic fashion. This is already beginning to emerge Western Europe, a fact which poses major challenges to the democratic systems of these societies.

Since *political* integration is the final bastion for immigrants, in terms of the right to vote and to stand for election, the implication is in practice a significant limitation in representative democracy (Hammar 1990). A substantial proportion of the adult work force in many European countries is

---

98. In the Flemish part of Belgium an agreement has now been reached which authorizes enrolling children of foreigners without legal residence in Flemish schools. According to the Minister of Education, this is merely a matter of regularizing an already existing situation (*Migration News Sheet* August 1994).

neither represented nor heard in political contexts. There are actually *millions* of people in Europe who are part of the economy, but not the polity (Tung 1981).

In consequence, the opinions and interests of immigrants are not articulated through democratic channels. Conversely, since immigrants are not seen as political actors, politicians do not feel they have to "pander to" these groups in the same way as to the citizens.[99] On the other hand, attitudes among the *native* population in relation to immigration will attract the attention of politicians. In this respect politicians play a central role, whether they act to reflect, reinforce or transcend the public sentiment. Despite the possible deeper causes, immigration has *de facto* become a public target for dissent, in turn pushing politicians into a constituency trap. Being responsive to voter expectations, politicians may – subtly or more openly – serve as "reinforcers" of hostile tendencies, thus inducing new demands for restrictions and control. When unintended consequences proliferate, the policy makers tend to get into what D. Papademetriou (1991) calls a "crisis-management mode", which in many ways is counter-productive to accommodation of the problem. Public attention is aroused and serves to strengthen crisis perceptions of the problem. Extreme reactions may surface like *le Pen's* National Front in France and the new extreme Right elsewhere in Europe, which again limits the space available to the authorities for manoeuvring. Beside the extremist parties which flourish on immigration issues, the *responsible* parties in Europe also become more restrictive, coupled with substantial avoidance symptoms as to deeper causes of population movements and xenophobic tendencies. These "avoidance symptoms" might in turn let the arena open for actors who connect "the decline of the welfare state" with pressure imposed by immigration. The nemesis in the situation is the growing credibility problem due to the apparent debilitation of the political community.

---

99. In Frankfurt – the German city with the highest proportion of immigrants (more than 20%) – voting rights for established foreigners would increase the voting population by more than 15% (Faist 1993).

Controlling economic consequences of immigration

Labour market considerations in relation to immigration are basically a question of controlling the consequences of immigration.

The linkages between labour-market structure and immigration are complex and historically specific. Extensive immigration may, under certain conditions, boost the economy by alleviating bottlenecks, and thereby increase the profit rate. This may further promote investments in technology, which again may facilitate restructuring. On the other hand, it is often argued, comprehensive and lasting immigration may discourage investments in labour-saving technology, as long as "cheap labour" is abundant.

However, even if scholars would agree as to the "objective" functioning of immigration in receiving economies, the market forces of migration, as well as the ineffective control systems, would have an independent momentum beyond the planning procedures of governments. One reason for this is that there are inconsistencies in the market needs of receiving countries. Despite recurrent unemployment, certain sectors of the European economies seem to be short of labour, seasonally and more permanently. This applies particularly to agriculture, hotel and catering, construction, small sub-contracting firms, maintenance and cleaning, as well as various other services (Commission 1992c).

Even though all member countries are overwhelmingly in favour of restricting immigration, certain EU states (Germany, France, Luxembourg, Spain, and Italy) nevertheless want to keep the door open for a policy of labour immigration. Through arrangements like short-term contract work, quotas, etc.,[100] these governments hope to keep some flexibility in re-

---

100. Daniéle Joly has in this context even indicated the new institution of "temporary protection" of refugees, triggered off by the crisis in former Yugoslavia, as a potential source of temporary labour which will (intentionally) not imply permanent settlement (Joly 1993).

lation to needs in the labour market, while at the same time retaining a restrictive general immigration policy.

This brings us back to Figure 1 (page 8) and the question of why it has been so difficult to harmonize the immigration policies of the member countries of the European Union.

Chapter 8

Internal Variation and Common Dilemmas. Concluding Remarks

It has been the intension of this book to spell out and analyse the complex interaction between economic, political, and emotional forces in the context of current immigration to Europe. The importance of approaching the field analytically as a whole has been stressed, as one migration tide may be a function of another. Also, the need to understand both the structural causes of migration and the individual motivations and aspirations of those who actually move – the macro-micro connections in migration – needs to be underscored. Basically migration is a question of *relations* – individually, institutionally, and internationally. This implies that the phenomenon also has to be addressed at many levels simultaneously. The issue is placed in the intersection between humanitarian obligations and economic/political considerations. It touches upon global questions of solidarity and it relates to the normative basis for the welfare state.

Current immigration to Europe is clearly demonstrating how dependent the different receiving states are on their respective policies. The popular movements are results of global tendencies that call for international cooperation and decision making: the population increase; ecological imbalances; the welfare gap North–South; political tensions and open conflicts are all factors that underline the interconnectedness of the phenomenon and the mutual dependence of the various actors on the international scene. The globalisation of the market place has made the nation-state dependent on economic and political processes outside its borders to an accelerating degree over the last decades. The question of national control is loosing currency in this setting where events and processes are increasingly inter-dependent; where supra-national decision making is gaining ground; where trans-national corporations for long have reduced the power of nation-states; and where international transportation and satellite media are making news coverage of the world continuously easier.

It is therefore somewhat a paradox that in such a situation, governments entrench themselves in national control systems in relation to immigration; tightening up border control; reinforcing the internal alien control systems; embarking upon bilateral labour contracts with third countries, and retaining sovereignty in terms of defining welfare provisions, labour market corollaries and other integrative measures pertaining to immigrants.

The dual dynamics

Concerning immigration, the nation-states within the European Community find themselves in a dual dynamics, related on the one hand to the internal national complex where control policies, integration efforts, and labour market parameters interact, and, on the other hand, to the international complex where the European integration process constitutes the paramount order.

The particular configuration of the forces contained in the triangle of Figure 6 (page 147) will constitute the *national* immigration complex of each of the receiving countries. As we have seen, the structure of the labour market (in terms of composition of demand, unemployment, size of unofficial market, etc.) will influence the size and composition of actual immigration, while this structure is in turn influenced by immigration. Thus, directly and indirectly, entry control and internal control mechanisms have an impact on labour market factors, as the structural labour demand will constitute important preconditions for effective control.

Labour market facilities are furthermore a central variable in the matter of *integration*. Wage labour opens up other doors to society. Conversely, lack of integration will easily imply marginalization which might, in turn, affect the structure of the labour market.

Figure 6. The European immigration complex

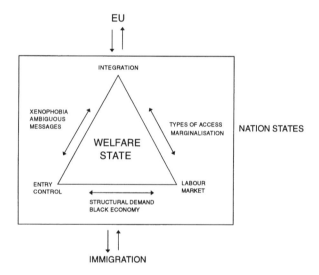

Concerning the interaction between *integration* and immigration *control*, one rather obvious relation has been discussed, in the sense that lack of entry and internal control hampers planning, and thus complicates integration into advanced welfare states. Deficient integration of immigrants would therefore tend to influence entry control policies in more restrictive directions. A more subtle mechanism in between control and integration related to the ambiguous implicit messages is contained in restrictive control policies: Having heavy restrictions on immigration could be interpreted as official authorization of the insider/outsider "us"/"them" thinking, which contributes to worsening the climate rather than alleviating relations between already established immigrants and nationals.

These complex internal dynamics in the respective nation-states impede coherent planning and policy formulation. Furthermore, any total "fencing-out" of third-country immigrants is untenable, for many reasons. Apart from control aspects – the "hole in the fence" problems – and inconsistent market needs, basic humanitarian or moral aspects are involved in the issue, which here has been discussed in terms of welfare-state dilemmas.

Beyond the inherent nation-state quandaries, the international setting constitutes the outer context with which nation-states also have to interact. On the one hand, the national configuration affects the room for manoeuvre for other European countries and for the European Community as such. On the other hand, the European integration process has an indirect and direct (although still limited) impact on the national momentum.

Real and perceived pressures

The nation-state has in Europe today come under pressure from "above" through the urge towards harmonization, and from "below" in terms of increased immigration. This double squeeze has led to a feeling of insecurity among much of the population, which again makes it more difficult for the states to agree to relinquish sovereignty. The national authorities instead find it important to signal decisiveness and control within traditionally defined boundaries and a familiar system for decision making.

The issue of national identity is the hidden agenda in this field. Originally the psychological counterpart of the nation-building processes that took place in Europe after the French Revolution, it has currently, in Western Europe, entered a defensive mode.

It was not until Denmark rejected the Maastricht Treaty in 1992, closely followed by a large and negative French minority, that European politicians seriously realized that the Union project had developed too fast at best. According to the Danish social scientist, Ulf Hedetoft (*Information* 18 September 1992), the Danes rejected the Treaty because they sensed that the Union represented a "cultural threat to self-determination and sovereignty" and that it would thwart those relations on which national identity depends.

The Danish case can be seen as a miniature example of the general problems confronting Europe in the relations between populations and political actors. Political and economic integration presupposes integration at the level of consciousness – a decomposition of mental frontiers and cultural space, which has failed to take place to any significant degree. The political process has become disconnected from the cultural environment and from popular sentiment.

By giving away sovereignty, as well as opening national borders, people might develop a feeling of insecurity as to responsibility of decision making in the realm of national interests and well-being. Parts of the decision making and politics are moved from the national arena to the European level, without the simultaneous creation of a "European people". "A *Zollverein* is not a *patrie*", as Ernest Renan phrased it more than a hundred years ago (Renan [1882]1990:18). Essentially there seems to be a dialectic relation between internationalization and identity protection/reformation. Establishing a framework for identity at the supra-national level will necessarily take time. It may also be that a reconsolidation of *national* identities is a necessary intermediary (or more lasting) stage on the road. The outcome of this process is far from obvious today. Even if the nation-state bastion may gradually give way to supra-national structures, the identity issue might well settle on lower levels of the scale.

The effects of the Community supra-nation-building process on nationhood and national identity represents the "squeeze of nationhood" from above. The squeeze from below

– from real and perceived immigration pressure – might prove even more significant when it comes to popular perceptions of a threat to the established order.[101]

One may discuss the probability and realism in the scenarios on which threat perceptions are built. Among experts there seems to be near consensus that both politicians and the media tend to dramatize the prospects.[102] Historical parallels are drawn to show that the *de facto* flows of today by no means are alarming compared to earlier phases in Europe. Besides, immigration "pressure" is obviously also a function of how strictly border control is enforced: As long as foreign labour was in demand, immigration pressure was not an issue in the West.

However, this has little to say for popular reactions, as long as social definitions are in accordance with the alarm scenario. If immigration is perceived as a threat, it *becomes* a threat, until the public can be convinced of the contrary. It is in the end the *feeling* of being swamped, as well as worries in relation to the unpredictability of the future, that substantiate general anxiety over immigration.

Concerning xenophobia and racism, it is hard to come to grips with the causal versus consequential aspects, as facts *are created* along the way. Gunnar Myrdal's classic study (1964) on white American discriminatory behaviour towards blacks is illustrative in this respect. His theory presupposes that the white population historically has believed itself to be superior, which then made it seem reasonable to discriminate the blacks. As a consequence, blacks are disadvantaged in the competition for goods in society, which leads in turn to underachievement, thereby verifying the basis for the discrimination in the first place. As the blacks are treated as inferior, they become inferior.

---

101. A recent survey in the former DDR revealed that people believed 30–40% of the current population were immigrants. The real figure is close to 1% (*Information* 2 July 1993).
102. See Dittgen 1992; Miller 1991; and Silverman 1992 among others.

If we interpret Myrdal's theory in today's European context, the question of "superiority" can be replaced by "having priority", legitimized by "ownership to territory" by birth and membership in a welfare society. We have argued that such exclusive processes are more likely to be activated when economic recession threatens established welfare standards for larger parts of the population – or again – when recession is *felt* to be threatening.

The "stop" policy introduced by Western European governments during the 1970s was an attempt to curtail immigration, and also stem the social and political unrest attached to perceptions of a continuous influx.

As we have seen, immigration to Western Europe has in fact increased (with some fluctuations) since the "stop" was effectuated. This has been due to system weaknesses as well as the politico-physical limitations of control. For one thing, the streams of migrants have changed character, partly in response to the "stop policy", which again has reduced the relevance of the very same policy. Secondly, physical control possibilities are related to political legitimacy in an intricate way. Migrants manage to penetrate most borders, unless the authorities are ready to militarize them. There is, however, a fear that militarizing external borders may eventually lead to the militarization of *society* as well, and consequently the subversion of the democratic tradition. This essential threshold is, of course, impossible to determine. In liberal societies there is no clear cutting-edge where control turns into repression. The point here has been to elucidate some of the dangers in such a *process*; the intrinsic subtle relations between immigration control, social structures, and democratic ideals.

"Dialectics of control"

International migration represents a dynamic system, where cumulative processes of actors, groups of actors, institutions, as well as political and economic structures interplay in a complex web. Economic, social, and cultural changes generated in both areas of origin and destination through international migration, equip the flows of people with a forceful inherent momentum not easily regulated by governments.

This brings us back to the question of "dialectics of control" introduced in the first section: Control strategies imposed by the authorities of receiving countries tend to give rise to counter-strategies or strategies of circumvention by actual and potential migrants. Immigrants are *actors* who will react to restrictive policies by utilizing whatever channels are available. Networks, in terms of established immigrant populations, play a central role in this respect, functioning as a linkage for both legal and illegal immigrants into the receiving society and the labour market during the initial phase of the establishment.

International migration is by no means a *solely* positive or negative phenomenon. As a social fact throughout the history of mankind, it has to be analysed within a specific historical context. In today's Western Europe, fears of a mass influx at times distort a sober analysis of migration issues, and nourish a more short-sighted approach. The "Fortress Europe" metaphor reflects the most rigid anticipation of how policies may become in Europe. Yet, in G. Tapinos's words, "democratic countries cannot do whatever they like" (1991), – and "whatever they like" is also, as we have seen, a contradictory realm.

References

Ad Hoc Group on Immigration (1991), *Report from the Ministers Responsible for Immigration to the European Council Meeting in Maastricht on Immigration and Asylum Policies*, SN 4038/91 (WGI 930), Brussels, 3 December.

Amersfoort, Hans van and Rinus Penninx (1994), "Regulating migration in Europe: The Dutch experience, 1960–92", *The Annals of The American Academy of Political and Social Science*, vol. 534, July.

Anderson, Benedict (1992), *Imagined Communities*, London and New York: Verso.

Barsotti, Odo and Laura Lecchini (1992), *Social and Economic Aspects of Foreign Immigration into Italy*, paper presented at IAS/IIASA conference Mass Migration in Europe. Implications in East and West, Vienna, March 5–7.

Birmingham City Council (1991), *1992 and Race Equality. Fact Pack*, Birmingham.

Blaschke, Jochen (1989), "Refugees and Turkish migrants in West Berlin", in D. Joly and R. Cohen (eds.), *Reluctant Hosts: Europe and its Refugees*, Aldershot: Avebury.

Blotevogel, Hans Heinrich, Ursula Müller-ter Jung and Gerald Wood (1993), "From itinerant worker to immigrant? The geography of guestworkers in Germany", in R. King (ed.).

Brochmann, Grete (1993), *Middle East Avenue. Female Migration from Sri Lanka to the Gulf*, Boulder, Colo.: Westview Press.

Brox, Ottar (1991), *Jeg er ikke rasist, men ... Hvordan får vi våre meninger om innvandrere og innvandring?*, Oslo: Gyldendal.

Brubaker, Rogers (1992), *Citizenship and Nationhood in France and Germany*, Cambridge, Mass.: Harvard University Press.

Böhning, W.R. and J. Werquin (1990), "Réflexions d'ordre économique, social et sur les droits de l'homme concernant le futur statut des nationaux des pays tiers dans le marché intérieur européen", *ILO Working Paper*, Geneva.

Calhoun, Craig (1992), *Why Nationalism? Sovereignty, Societal Integration and Identity in a World System of States*, paper presented at the Norwegian National Sociology Conference, Lofoten, June 17–21.

Callovi, Giuseppe (1990), *Regulating Immigration in the European Community. Effects of the Single European Act upon Migration Policies and on the Decision-Making Process in the Area*, lecture given at the International Conference of Europeanists, Washington DC, March 23–24.

Callovi, Giuseppe (1992), "Regulation of immigration in 1993: pieces of the European Community jig-saw puzzle", *International Migration Review*, vol. 26, no. 98, Summer.

Carens, Joseph H. (1987), "Aliens and citizens: The case for open borders", *The Review of Politics*, vol. 49, no. 2.

Castles, Stephen (1986), "The guest-worker in Western Europe – an obituary", *International Migration Review*, vol. 20, no. 4.

Chesnais, Jean-Claude (1990), *Migration from Eastern to Western Europe, Past (1946–1989) and Future (1990–2000)*, paper presented for the Council of Europe, Strasbourg, September.

Chesnais, Jean-Claude (1991), *The USSR Emigration. Past, Present and Future*, paper presented at the International Conference on Migration, Rome, March 13–15.

Christensen, Arne Piel and Morten Kjærum (1991), "Myter og virkelighet i flyktningdebatten", *Mennesker og rettigheter*, nr. 1.

Cohen, Robin (1987), *The New Helots. Migrants in the International Division of Labour*, Aldershot: Gower.

Commission of the European Communities (1988), *Communication of the Commission on the Abolition of Controls of Persons at Intra-Community Borders*, COM (88) 640 final, Brussels.

Commission of the European Communities (1990), *Policies on Immigration and the Social Integration of Migrants in the European Community*, SEC (90) 1813 final, Brussels, 28 September.

Commission of the European Communities (1991), *Commission Communication to the Council and the European Parliament on Immigration*, SEC (91) 1855 final, Brussels, 23 October.

Commission of the European Communities (1992a), *Commission Communication to the Council and to Parliament on the Abolition of Border Controls*, SEC (92) 877 final, Brussels, 8 May.

Commission of the European Communities (1992b), *Immigration Policies in the Member-States: Between the Need for Control and the Desire for Integration*, Summary report from the Information Network on Migrations from Non-Member States (RIMET), Brussels, May.

Commission of the European Communities (1992c), *Immigration and Employment*, Working Paper, SEC (92) 955, Brussels, May 7.

Commission of the European Communities (1993), *Immigration – the Sit-*

uation in the EC Member States in 1992. Attitudes Towards Controls, La-bour Market Requirements and the Challenge of Integration, General report by the Information Network on Migrations from Non-Member States (RIMET), Brussels, June.

Commission of the European Communities (1994), *Communication from the Commission to the Council and the European Parliament*, COM (94) 23 Final, Brussels, 23 February.

Cornelius, Wayne A., Philip L. Martin and James F. Hollifield (1994), *Controlling Immigration. A Global Perspective*. Stanford, Calif.: Stanford University Press.

Council of Europe (1990), *Migratory Movements from Central and East European Countries to Western Europe – Some Selected Aspects*, Strasbourg MMP-HF (90) 6.

Crowley, John (1992), *Ethnicity, Democratic Theory and the Nation-State*, paper presented at the IAS/IIASA/IF conference, Mass Migration in Europe. Implications in East and West, Vienna, March 5–7.

Cruz, Antonio (1991a), "Current trends and developments. Will the European Community make the 1992 deadline on the abolition of internal border controls?", *Quarterly Review of the International Organization for Migration*, vol. 29, no. 3, September.

Cruz, Antonio (1991b), *Community Competence over Third-Country Nationals Residing in an EC Member-State*, Briefing Paper no. 5, Churches Committee for Migrants in Europe, Brussels.

Cruz, Antonio (1993), *Schengen, Ad Hoc Immigration Group and Other European Intergovernmental Bodies*, Briefing Paper no. 12, Churches Committee for Migrants in Europe, Brussels.

Culpitt, Ian (1992), *Welfare and Citizenship. Beyond the Crisis of the Welfare State?*, London: Sage.

Dittgen, Herbert (1992), *What is a European? Citizenship and Immigration in Europe*, paper presented at the Council for European Studies, Eighth International Conference of Europeanists, Chicago, March 27–29.

Dummet, Ann and Jan Niessen (1993), *Immigration and Citizenship in the European Union*, CCME Briefing Paper no. 14.

EEC Treaty (1987), *Treaties Establishing the European Communities*, Luxembourg: ECSC, EEC, EAEC.

Entzinger, Han and Jack Carter (1989), "New immigration and the role of the state", in Han Entzinger and Jack Carter (eds.), *International Review of Comparative Public Policy*, vol. 1, A Research Annual, Immigration in Western Democracies: The United States and Western Europe, Greenwich, Conn. and London: Jai Press.

Enzensberger, Hans M. (1992), "Remarks on the Great Migration", in *Framtider*, vol. 2, Institute for Future Studies, Stockholm, pp. 14–18.

European Parliament (1991), *On the Free Movement of Persons and Security in the European Community*, DOC_DA\RR\112531\brp.

European Parliament (1992), *Second Report of the Committee on Civil Lib-*

erties and Internal Affairs on the Entry into Force of the Schengen Agreement, DOC_EN\RR\216\216495.WP5.

Faist, Thomas (1993), How to Define a Foreigner? The Symbolic Politics of Immigration in German Partisan Discourse, 1978–1992, Zentrum für Sozialpolitik – Arbeitspapier no. 12.

Faist, Thomas (1994), Boundaries of the Welfare State. Immigrants and Social Rights on the National and Supranational Level, unpublished paper, University of Bremen.

Fielding, Anthony (1993), "Mass migration and economic restructuring", in R. King (ed.).

Fijalkowski, Jürgen (1993), "Aggressive nationalism, immigration pressure and asylum policy disputes in contemporary Germany", International Migration Review, vol. 27, no. 104.

Flyktningerådet (1994), "Den globale flyktningesituasjon – bakgrunn, tall og tendenser," Flyktning, Oslo, January.

Freeman, Gary P. (1979), Immigrant Labour and Racial Conflict in Industrial Societies. The French and British Experience 1945–1975, Princeton, NJ: Princeton University Press.

Freeman, Gary P. (1986), "Migration and the political economy of the welfare state," The Annals of the American Academy of Political and Social Science, May.

Freeman, Gary P. (1992), "Migration policy and politics in the receiving states", International Migration Review, vol. 26, Winter, no. 4.

Garcia, Soledad (1992), Europe's Fragmented Identities and the Frontiers of Citizenship, Discussion Paper no. 45, London: The Royal Institute of International Affairs.

Ghosh, Bimal (1992), "Migratory movements from Central and East European countries to Western Europe", in Council of Europe, People on the Move. New Migration Flows in Europe, Strasbourg: Council of Europe Press.

Giddens, Anthony (1985), The Nation-State and Violence, Cambridge: Polity Press.

Gieseck, Arne Ullrich Heilemann and Hans D. von Loeffelholz (eds.) (1994), "Economic implications of migration into the Federal Republic of Germany 1988–1992", in S. Spencer (ed.).

Giorgi, Liana, Ronald Pohoryles, Sabine Pohoryles-Drexel and Gabriele Schmid (1992), "The internal logic and contradictions of migration control: An excursion into theory and practice in relation to East–West migration", Innovation in Social Sciences Research, vol. 5, no. 3.

Golini, A., G. Gerano and F. Heins (1991), "South–North migration with special reference to Europe", International Migration, vol. 29, no. 2.

Hammar, Tomas (1990), Democracy and the Nation-State, Aldershot: Avebury.

Hammar, Tomas, (ed.) (1985), European Immigration Policy. A Comparative Study, London: Cambridge University Press.

Heisler, Barbara S. (1992), "The future of immigrant incorporation: Which models? Which concepts?", *International Migration Review*, vol. 26, Summer.

Heisler, M.O. and B. Heisler (1990), "Citizenship – old, new and changing", in H. Fijalkowski et al. (eds.), *Dominant National Cultures and Ethnic Identities*, Berlin: Free University.

Hernes, Gudmund and K. Knudsen (1990), *Svart på hvitt. Norske reaksjoner på flyktninger, asylsøkere og innvandrere*, Oslo: FAFO.

Hollifield, James F. (1986), "Immigration policy in France and Germany: Outputs versus outcomes", *Annals of the American Academy of Political and Social Sciences*, May.

Hollifield, James F. (1992), *Immigrants, Markets and States. The Political Economy of Post-War Europe*, Cambridge, Mass.: Harvard University Press.

Hovy, Béla (1992), *Asylum Migration in Europe: Patterns, Determinants and the Role of East–West Movements*, paper presented at the IAS/-IIASA conference, Mass migration in Europe. Implications in East and West, Vienna, March 5–7.

Hönekopp, Elmar (1991), *Migratory Movements from Countries of Central and Eastern Europe: Causes and Characteristics, Present Situation and Possible Future Trends – The Cases of Germany and Austria*, Council of Europe, Strasbourg.

Hylland Eriksen, Thomas (1991), *Veien til et mer eksotisk Norge. En bok om nordmenn og andre underlige folkeslag*, Oslo: Ad Notam.

ILO (1989), *Informal Consultation Meeting on Migrants from Non-EEC Countries in the Single European Market after 1992*, Informal Summary Record, Geneva 27–28 April.

Joly, Daniele (1993), *The Porous Dam: European Harmonization on Asylum in the Nineties*, paper presented at COST A2 workshop, Oslo, 19–21 November.

Kapteyn, Paul (1991), "'Civilization under negotiations'. National civilizations and European integration: The Treaty of Schengen", *European Journal of Sociology*, 32.

Kapteyn, Paul (1992), *A Stateless Market. National Civilizations and European Integration. Two Examples: EC Fraud and the Treaty of Schengen*, Institute Paper, Institute of Sociology, University of Amsterdam.

King, Mike (1992), "The impact of EC border policies on the policing of 'refugees' in Eastern and central Europe", *Innovation in Social Science Research*, vol. 5, no. 3.

King, Russell (ed.) (1993), *Mass Migration in Europe. The Legacy and the Future*, London: Belhaven Press.

Kitching, Gavin (1985), "Nationalism: The instrumental passion", *Capital and Class*, no. 25, Spring, pp. 98–114.

Layton-Henry, Zig (1984), *The Politics of Race in Britain*, London: George Allen and Unwin.

Layton-Henry, Zig (1990), "The challenge of political rights", in Z. Layton-Henry (ed.).

Layton-Henry, Zig (ed.) (1990), *The Political Rights of Migrant Workers in Western Europe*, London: Sage.

Leca, Jean (1992), "Nationalité et citoyenneté dans l'Europe des immigrations", in J. Costa-Lascoux and P. Weil (eds.), *Logiques d'états et immigrations*, Paris: Éditions Kime.

Livi Bacci, Massimo (1991), *South–North Migration: A Comparative Approach to North American and European Experiences*, paper presented at the OECD International Conference on migration, Rome, 13–15 March.

Loescher, Gil (1989), "EC policy on refugees", *International Affairs*, vol. 65, no. 4.

Maddison, Angus (1991), *Dynamic Forces in Capitalist Development. A Long-Run Comparative Review*, Oxford: Oxford University Press.

Marie, Claude-Valentin (1987), *Migrants in Western Europe: Present Situation and Future Prospects. Clandestine Migration and Unauthorised Migrants in Council of Europe Member States*, MMG-3 (87) 2, Strasbourg: Council of Europe.

Marie, Claude-Valentin (1991), *Immigration et democratie*, unpublished paper, Paris.

Marshall, Gordon (ed.) (1994), *The Concise Oxford Dictionary of Sociology*, Oxford: Oxford University Press.

Martin, P.L., E. Hönekopp, and H. Ullmann (1991), "Conference Report: Europe 1992, effects on labour migration", *International Migration Review*, 24.

Massey, Douglas S. et al. (1993), "Theories of international migration: A review and appraisal", *Population and Development Review*, vol. 19, no. 3, pp. 431–466.

Mehrländer, Ursula (1994), "The development of post-war migration and refugee policy", in S. Spencer (ed.).

Miller, Mark (1991), *The Future of International Migration to Western Europe*, paper presented to the American Political Science Association Convention, Washington DC, 30 August.

Miller, Mark and Christopher Mitchell (1993), *Comparing Policy-Making Patterns Towards Migration in Industrial Democracies: Western Europe and the United States*, paper presented at a seminar on migration, Center for Latin American and Caribbean Studies, New York University, February 26.

Myrdal, Gunnar (1964), *An American Dilemma*. New York: Harper and Brothers.

OECD (1990), *SOPEMI 1989. Continuous Reporting System on Migration*, Directorate for Social Affairs, Manpower and Education, Paris.

OECD (1991), *SOPEMI 1990* (OCDE/GD(91)129).

OECD (1992), *SOPEMI. Trends in International Migration*. Annual Report, Paris.

OECD (1993), *SOPEMI. Trends in International Migration*. Annual Report, Paris.

OECD (1995), *SOPEMI. Trends in International Migration.* Annual Report, (1994), Paris.

Ogden, Philip (1993), "The legacy of migration: Some evidence from France", in R. King (ed.).

Okolski, Marek (1990), *Migratory Movements from Countries of Central and Eastern Europe*, paper presented at a Council of Europe meeting, Strasbourg, November.

Okolski, Marek (1991), *Migratory Movements from Countries of Central and Eastern Europe*, Council of Europe Conference, Vienna.

Papademetriou, Demetrios (1991), *Confronting the Challenge of Transnational Migration: Domestic and International Responses*, paper presented at the International Conference on Migration, OECD, Rome, 5–7 March.

Piore, Michael J. (1979), *Birds of Passage. Migrant Labour and Industrial Societies*, London: Cambridge University Press.

Portes, Alejandro and Jozsef Böröcz (1989), "Contemporary immigration: Theoretical perspectives on its determinants and modes of incorporation", *International Migration Review*, vol. 23, no. 87.

Portes, Alejandro and Patricia F. Kelly (1989), "Images of movement in a changing world: A review of current theories of international migration", in H. Entzinger and J. Carter (eds.).

Renan, Ernest ([1882] 1990), "What is a nation?", in Homi Bhabha (ed.), *Nation and Narration*, London: Routledge.

Rogers, Rosemary (1985), *Guests Come to Stay. The Effects of European Labour Migration on Sending and Receiving Countries*, Boulder, Colo./London: Westview Press.

Rokkan, Stein (1974), " Entries, voices, exits: Towards a possible generalization of the Hirschman model", *Social Science Information*, vol. 13, no. 1.

Rudolph, Hedwig and Sabine Hübner (1993), "Repatriates – guest workers and immigrants: Legacies and challenges for German politics," in H. Rudolph and M. Morokwasic (eds.), *Bridging States and Markets, International Migration in the Early 1990s*, Berlin: Edition Sigma WZB, pp. 265–289.

Rystad, Göran (1992), "Immigration history and the future of international migration", *International Migration Review*, vol. 26, no. 4.

Salt, John (1989), "A comparative overview of international trends and types, 1950–80", *International Migration Review*, vol. 23, no. 87.

Salt, John (1992), "Current and future international migration trends affecting Europe", in Council of Europe, *People on the Move. New Migration Flows in Europe*, Strasbourg: Council of Europe Press.

Sciortino, Giuseppe (1990), *Immigration from Outside the EEC and Migratory Policies: The Perverse Effects of Policies Designed to Block Immigration*, paper presented at the 12th Congress of Sociology, Madrid, July.

Sciortino, Guiseppe (1991), "Immigration into Europe and public policy: Do stops really work?", *New Community*, vol. 18, no. 1.

Silverman, Maxim (1990), "The racialization of immigration: Aspects of discourse from 1968–1981", *French Cultural Studies*, vol. 1.

Silverman, Maxim (ed.) (1991), *Race, Discourse and Power in France*. Research in Ethnic Relations Series, Aldershot: Avebury.

Silverman, Maxim (1992), *Deconstructing a Nation. Immigration, Racism and Citizenship in Modern France*, London and New York: Routledge.

Soysal, Yasemin (1992), *European Community and Immigration*, unpublished paper, Department of Sociology, Harvard University.

Soysal, Yasemin (1993), *Construction(s) of Boundaries: Immigrant Identities in Europe*, paper presented at the Conference on European Identity and its Intellectual Roots, Cambridge, May 6–9.

Spencer, Sarah (ed.) (1994), *Immigration as an Economic Asset. The German Experience*. Staffordshire: IPPR Trentham Books.

Stalker, Peter (1994), *The Work of Strangers: A Survey of International Labour Migration*. Geneva: International Labour Office.

Stölting, Erhard (1991), "Festung Europa. Grenzziehungen in der Ost-West-Migration", *PROKLA*, vol. 21, no. 2.

Tapinos, George (1991), *Can International Cooperation be an Alternative to the Emigration of Workers?*, paper presented at the International Conference on Migration, OECD, Rome, 5–7 March.

Teitelbaum, Michael (1991), *The Effects of Economic Development on Out-Migration Pressures in Sending Countries*, paper presented at the International Conference on Migration, OECD, Rome, 5–7 March.

Tomasi, Lydio and Mark Miller (1993), "Post cold-war international migration to Western Europe: Neither fortress nor invasion", in M.B. Rocha-Trindade (ed.), *Recent Migration Trends in Europe*, Lisboa: Universidade Aberta, Instituto de Estudos para o Desenvolvimento.

Tung, Roger Ko-Chih (1981), *Exit-Voice Catastrophes. Dilemma Between Migration and Participation*, Stockholm Studies in Politics, 18, University of Stockholm.

Walzer, Michael (1983), *Spheres of Justice: Defence of Pluralism and Equality*. New York: Basic Books.

Weil, Patrick 1992, "Convergences et divergences des politiques de flux", in J. Costa-Lascoux and P. Weil (eds.), *Logiques d'états et immigration*, Kimé, Paris.

Widgren, Jonas (1993), *The Need for a New Multilateral Order to Prevent Mass Movements from Becoming a Security Threat in Europe*, paper presented at the conference New Mobilities – Element of European Integration, Berlin, 23–24 April.

Wieviorka, Michel (1992), *Popular and Political Racism in Europe. Unity and Diversity*, paper presented at the BSA Annual Conference, Canterbury, 23–24 April.

Wilpert, Czarina (1991), "Migration and ethnicity in a non-immigration country: Foreigners in a united Germany", *New Community*, vol. 18, no. 1.

Withol de Wenden, Catherine (1990), "The absence of rights: the position of illegal immigrants", in Z. Layton-Henry (ed.).

Woollacott, Martin (1992), "The politics of exclusion", in *Framtider*, vol. 2, Institute for Future Studies, Stockholm.

World Council of Churches (1991), *Refugees and Asylum Seekers in a Common European House*, Geneva, August.

Zimmermann, Klaus F. (1994), "The labour market impact of immigration», in S. Spencer (ed.).

Zolberg, Aristide (1983), "Contemporary transnational migrations in historical perspective: Patterns and dilemmas", in M. Kritz (ed.), *U.S. Immigration and Refugee Policy*, Lexington: D.C. Heath.

Østerberg, Dag (1988), *Metasociology. An Inquiry into the Origins and Validity of Social Thought*, Oslo: Norwegian University Press.

Ålund, Alexandra and Carl-Ulrik Schierup (eds.) (1991), *Paradoxes of Multiculturalism*, Aldershot: Avebury.

Index